Table of Contents

THE PLURAL

1) Singular **+ s**
   parrot – parrot**s**   apple – apple**s**   girl – girl**s**

2) Words **ending with y** if a consonant is written before ⇒ **ies**
   lol**ly** – lol**lies**   stor**y** – stor**ies**   strawber**ry** – strawberr**ies**
   But: boy – boys, bay – bays

3) Words **ending with ch, x, s, sh, o** ⇒ **es**
   clas**s** – class**es**   bo**x** – box**es**   brus**h** – brush**es**

4) Some words **ending with f, fe, lf** ⇒ **ves**
   kni**fe** – kni**ves**   wol**f** – wol**ves**   li**fe** – li**ves**
   But: chiefs, safes, cliffs, handkerchiefs

5) **Irregular forms**

man – men	woman – women	tooth – teeth	foot – feet
mouse – mice	child – children	goose – geese	ox – oxen
louse – lice	person - people	sheep - sheep	deer - deer
bison - bison	fish - fish	moose - moose	offspring - offspring

You can use **singular or plural** with words like family, class, police, team, army, band, choir, class, club, crew, company, firm, gang, government, orchestra, party, staff, etc.

In British English the plural is used more often than in American English.

If the group acts in unison (as a group), use a **singular verb**:

My family **lives** in Miami.   All the members living under one roof.
The team **was** successful.   You see the team as a group.

If the group acts individually, use a **plural verb**:

My family **live** in towns all over Florida.   Each individual is living a separate life in
                                                  a different town.

The team **were** successful.   You see the single members of the team

PLURAL 1

child		potato	
party		toy	
boy		key	
fish		ox	
desk		kiss	
toffee		life	
book		lady	
woman		calf	
apple		knife	
star		tooth	
trolley		family	
toe		day	
cow		phone	
house		bear	
photo		brush	
glass		wolf	
pen		strawberry	
car		monkey	
baby		man	
thief		foot	

PLURAL 2

Write down the number and the plural of the following words.

Example: a sister - 2 **two sisters**

an apple	5	an hour	6
a city	3	a lady	7
a box	10	a life	2
a brush	4	a tooth	10
a kiss	2	a key	4
a monkey	3	a fox	2
a strawberry	6	a baby	3
an orange	7	a goose	10
a family	12	a foot	2
a boy	11	a box	12
a player	8	a match	5
a man	2	a camera	11
a day	3	a bay	4
a knife	5	a story	9
a glass	4	a team	8
a fly	6	a pencil	7
a child	3	a laptop	2
a wolf	8	a lady	6

PLURAL 1

child	**children**	potato	**potatoes**
party	**parties**	toy	**toys**
boy	**boys**	key	**keys**
fish	**fish**	ox	**oxen**
desk	**desks**	kiss	**kisses**
toffee	**toffees**	life	**lives**
book	**books**	lady	**ladies**
woman	**women**	calf	**calves**
apple	**apples**	knife	**knives**
star	**stars**	tooth	**teeth**
trolley	**trolleys**	family	**families**
toe	**toes**	day	**days**
cow	**cows**	phone	**phones**
house	**houses**	bear	**bears**
photo	**photos**	brush	**brushes**
glass	**pens**	wolf	**wolves**
pen	**glasses**	strawberry	**strawberries**
car	**cars**	monkey	**monkeys**
baby	**babies**	man	**men**
thief	**thieves**	foot	**feet**

PLURAL 2

an apple	five **apples**	an hour	six **hours**
a city	three **cities**	a lady	seven **ladies**
a box	ten **boxes**	a life	two **lives**
a brush	four **brushes**	a tooth	ten **teeth**
a kiss	two **kisses**	a key	four **keys**
a monkey	three **monkeys**	a fox	two **foxes**
a strawberry	six **strawberries**	a baby	three **babies**
an orange	seven **oranges**	a goose	ten **geese**
a family	twelve **families**	a foot	two **feet**
a boy	eleven **boys**	a box	twelve **boxes**
a player	eight **players**	a match	five **matches**
a man	two **men**	a camera	eleven **cameras**
a day	three **days**	a bay	four **bays**
a knife	five **knives**	a story	nine **stories**
a glass	four **glasses**	a team	eight **teams**
a fly	six **flies**	a pencil	seven **pencils**
a child	three **children**	a laptop	two **laptops**
a wolf	eight **wolves**	a lady	six **ladies**

PLURAL 3

Write the correct plural noun into the gaps.

1. Which Mediterranean _____ are the cleanest? (beach)

2. Do you like _____? (tomato)

3. How much do _____'s shoes cost? (child)

4. How many _____ does a cat have? (life)

5. Which three _____ are the largest in the world? (city)

6. What percentage of _____ has three kids? (family)

7. What are the best _____ you have ever been to? (party)

8. How many _____ should we write in a formal letter? (kiss)

9. What is the best way to keep _____ out of the house? (fly)

10. How much would it cost to buy four _____ of bread? (loaf)

11. How many _____ are there in your town? (church)

12. What do most _____ think about all day? (man)

13. How many _____ did King Henry VIII have? (wife)

14. Should _____ be allowed to use animals? (circus)

15. How many _____ do you eat? (mango)

16. How many _____ does a millipede have? (foot)

17. At what age do _____ usually start to walk? (baby)

18. How many stomachs do _____ have? (sheep)

19. How much do _____ cost per kilogram? (cherry)

20. Are you good at _____? (quiz)

PLURAL 4

Write the correct plural noun into the gaps.

1. How many _____ does your cat catch? (mouse)

2. They usually keep their winter clothes in _____. (box)

3. We saw some _____ on our way to the beach. (deer)

4. She bought two _____ in our online shop. (scarf)

5. Our uncle often tells us funny _____. (story)

6. We often have _____ for dinner on Fridays. (fish)

7. My sister likes ice cream with _____. (blueberry)

8. Our dog has never had any _____. (louse)

9. The girls bought three _____ in the mall. (dress)

10. How many _____ work in your office? (person)

11. The farmer has a lot of _____ and oxen. (sheep / ox)

12. You should always keep your _____ warm in winter. (foot)

13. Does a cat really have seven _____? (life)

14. At how many _____ have you been this year? (party)

15. _____ broke into their house and stole some paintings. (thief)

16. You should clean your _____ twice a day. (tooth)

17. How many _____ work in the restaurant? (woman)

18. My brother always has two _____ for lunch. (sandwich)

19. He was unlucky because he missed the hole by _____. (inch)

20. They have five _____, three girl and two boys. (child)

Complete English Grammar Rules

PLURAL 3

1. Which Mediterranean **beaches** are the cleanest?
2. Do you like **tomatoes**?
3. How much do **children's** shoes cost?
4. How many **lives** does a cat have?
5. Which three **cities** are the largest in the world?
6. What percentage of **families** has three kids?
7. What are the best **parties** you have ever been to?
8. How many **kisses** should we write in a formal letter?
9. What is the best way to keep **flies** out of the house?
10. How much would it cost to buy four **loaves** of bread?
11. How many **churches** are there in your town?
12. What do most **men** think about all day?
13. How many **wives** did King Henry VIII have?
14. Should **circuses** be allowed to use animals?
15. How many **mangoes** do you eat?
16. How many **feet** does a millipede have?
17. At what age do **babies** usually start to walk?
18. How many stomachs do **sheep** have?
19. How much do **cherries** cost per kilogram?
20. Are you good at **quizzes**?

PLURAL 4

1. How many **mice** does your cat catch? (mouse)
2. They usually keep their winter clothes in **boxes**. (box)
3. We saw some **deer** on our way to the beach. (deer)
4. She bought two **scarves** in our online shop. (scarf)
5. Our uncle often tells us funny **stories**. (story)
6. We often have **fish** for dinner on Fridays. (fish)
7. My sister likes ice cream with **blueberries**. (blueberry)
8. Our dog has never had any **lice**. (louse)
9. The girls bought three **dresses** in the mall. (dress)
10. How many **people** work in your office? (person)
11. The farmer has a lot of **sheep** and **oxen**. (sheep / ox)
12. You should always keep your **feet** warm in winter. (foot)
13. Does a cat really have seven **lives**? (life)
14. At how many **parties** have you been this year? (party)
15. **Thieves** broke into their house and stole some paintings. (thief)
16. You should clean your **teeth** twice a day. (tooth)
17. How many **women** work in the restaurant? (woman)
18. My brother always has two **sandwiches** for lunch. (sandwich)
19. He was unlucky because he missed the hole by **inches**. (inch)
20. They have five **children**, three girl and two boys. (child)

COMMANDS

Commands are also known as **imperative forms**. They are easy to use. Put the verb in the base form at the beginning of the sentence and end the sentence with an object.

Tell someone to do something:

Put out the rubbish.
Take an umbrella with you.
Turn off the TV.

If you want to make commands negative, put "**don't**" or "**do not**" before the verb.

Tell someone not to do something:

Don't shout at me.
Don't open the window.
Do not stay out too late.

If you want to use the **polite form** of a command, then add the word "please".

Polite form:

Please don't shout at me.
Please tell me your phone number.
Hand out the books, please.
Help me with the homework, please.

COMMANDS 1

Fill in the gaps with the correct words from the box. Some of these commands are negative (-).

help – phone – eat – go – leave – clean – sit – drink – close – take – tell – read

1. _____ your shoes.

2. _____ your emails in the lesson. (-)

3. Today's her birthday. _____ her, please.

4. _____ her my phone number. (-)

5. It's cold outside. _____ the window, please.

6. _____ her in the kitchen.

7. _____ ice cream in winter. (-)

8. _____ on the table. (-)

9. _____ your dirty boots outside.

10. _____ and drive. (-)

11. _____ them to the airport.

12. _____ through the park at night. (-)

COMMANDS 2

Fill in the gaps with the correct words from the box. Some of these commands are negative (-).

tidy – write – call – be – shut – sit – drive – stay – help – take – buy – turn

1. _____ afraid. (-)

2. _____ the bus to school.

3. _____ too fast. (-)

4. _____ a taxi, please.

5. _____ on the desk. (-)

6. _____ down the music.

7. _____ a new laptop. (-)

8. _____ your room before you leave.

9. _____ me in the garden.

10. _____ the door, please.

11. _____ out too late. (-)

12. _____ the sentence on the board.

COMMANDS 3

Make the commands **negative** by using "**don't**".

1. Drive her to the shopping mall.

   _____

2. Stop at the next gas station.

   _____

3. Put your books on the desk.

   _____

4. Water the plants.

   _____

5. Cross the street.

   _____

6. Tell him your address.

   _____

7. Take an umbrella with you.

   _____

8. Close the door.

   _____

9. Help her with the homework.

   _____

10. Tell them what happened yesterday.

   _____

COMMANDS 1

1. **Clean** your shoes.
2. **Don't read** your emails in the lesson.
3. Today's her birthday. **Phone** her, please.
4. **Don't tell** her my phone number. (-)
5. It's cold outside. **Close** the window, please.
6. **Help** her in the kitchen.
7. **Don't eat** ice cream in winter.
8. **Don't sit** on the table. (-)
9. **Leave** your dirty boots outside.
10. **Don't drink** and drive. (-)
11. **Take** them to the airport.
12. **Don't go** through the park at night. (-)

COMMANDS 2

1. **Don't be** afraid. (-)
2. **Take** the bus to school.
3. **Don't drive** too fast. (-)
4. **Call** a taxi, please.
5. **Don't sit** on the desk. (-)
6. **Turn** down the music.
7. **Don't buy** a new laptop. (-)
8. **Tidy** your room before you leave.
9. **Help** me in the garden.
10. **Shut** the door, please.
11. **Don't stay** out too late. (-)
12. **Write** the sentence on the board.

COMMANDS 3

1. **Don't drive** her to the shopping mall.
2. **Don't stop** at the next gas station.
3. **Don't put** your books on the desk.
4. **Don't water** the plants.
5. **Don't cross** the street.
6. **Don't tell** him your address.
7. **Don't take** an umbrella with you.
8. **Don't close** the door.
9. **Don't help** her with the homework.
10. **Don't tell** them what happened yesterday.

FORMS OF "TO BE"

Singular	Long form	Short form	Examples
1st person	I **am**	I**'m**	I am (I'm) late.
2nd person	you **are**	you**'re**	You are (you're) clever.
3rd person	he **is**	he**'s**	He is (he's) happy.
	she **is**	she**'s**	She is (she's) hungry.
	it **is**	it**'s**	It is (it's) cold.

Plural			
1st person	we **are**	we**'re**	We are (we're) late.
2nd person	you **are**	you**'re**	You are (you're) sleepy.
3rd person	they **are**	they**'re**	They are (they're) great.

NEGATIONS AND QUESTIONS

Singular	Negations	Questions
1st person	I **am not** (I'm not) late.	**Am I** late?
2nd person	You **are not** (you aren't) clever.	**Are you** clever?
3rd person	He **is not** (he isn't) happy.	**Is he** happy?
	She **is not** (she isn't) hungry.	**Is she** hungry?
	It **is not** (it isn't) cold.	**Is it** cold?

Plural		
1st person	We **are not** (we aren't) late.	**Are we** late?
2nd person	You **are not** (you aren't) sleepy.	**Are you** sleepy?
3rd person	They **are not** (they aren't) great.	**Are they** great?

FORMS OF "TO BE" 1

Fill in am, is or are.

1.   She _____ in the house.

2.   The dog and the cat _____ in the garden.

3.   The woman _____ behind a tree.

4.   I _____ Kevin.

5.   Carol and I _____ friends.

6.   It _____ black.

7.   My name _____ Bob.

8.   They _____ nice girls.

9.   The children _____ in the shop.

10. He _____ a teacher.

11. We _____ hungry.

12. Mrs Dixon _____ funny and nice.

13. I _____ twelve years old.

14. Jim and Cathy _____ at school.

15. The elephants _____ tired.

16. Mr Cooper _____ in the house.

17. The boys _____ in the park.

18. The mouse _____ in front of the hole.

19. Peter _____ a clever boy.

20. I _____ Sam.

FORMS OF "TO BE" 2

Fill in **am, is** or **are.**

1.   Mr Baker and I _____ friends.

2.   It _____ time for dinner.

3.   My name _____ Caroline.

4.   My rabbit and my cat _____ friends.

5.   They _____ very nice animals.

6.   Dog food _____ also good for cats.

7.   The children _____ in the garden.

8.   Can I have an apple? Yes, here you _____.

9.   Mrs Dixon _____ funny and nice.

10. I _____ ten years old.

11. The weather _____ very nice today.

12. I _____ not tired.

13. This ball _____ very heavy.

14. The dogs _____ hungry. Let's feed them.

15. Look! Carol _____ at home.

16. This castle _____ very old.

17. My brother and I _____ good football players.

18. Ann _____ at the supermarket and her children _____ at school.

19. I _____ a student. My sister _____ a teacher.

20. How _____ you?

FORMS OF "TO BE" 3

Fill in the negation of **am, is** or **are.**

1. Canada _____ a small country.

2. Ann _____ a nice girl.

3. My hands _____ cold.

4. They _____ tired.

5. He _____ a bad teacher.

6. I _____ at work.

7. She _____ at home in the morning.

8. We _____ in the park.

9. Jim _____ at school.

10. Our friends _____ on their summer holidays.

11. Uncle George _____ a good football player.

12. The dog _____ under the table.

13. He _____ very funny.

14. The shoes _____ white.

15. You _____ right.

16. Susan _____ good at tennis.

17. They _____ in the house.

18. His T-shirts _____ cool.

19. My sister _____ a good swimmer.

20. She _____ in Italy.

FORMS OF "TO BE" 4

Form the **questions** of the following sentences.

1.   They are at school.   _____

2.   She is lazy.   _____

3.   The boys are good at school.   _____

4.   Kevin is a good tennis player.   _____

5.   The elephants are tired.   _____

6.   Liam is good at Maths.   _____

7.   The book is on the desk.   _____

8.   You are rich.   _____

9.   His shoes are black.   _____

10. The cats are in the tree.   _____

11. I am late.   _____

12. They are busy.   _____

13. Pamela is pretty.   _____

14. The car is new.   _____

15. She is a nice girl.   _____

16. They are in the garden.   _____

17. My parents are at work.   _____

18. Tim is on holidays.   _____

19. It is a young cat.   _____

20. The books are in the schoolbag.   _____

FORMS OF "TO BE" 1

1. She **is** in the house.
2. The dog and the cat **are** in the garden.
3. The woman **is** behind a tree.
4. I **am** Kevin.
5. Carol and I **are** friends.
6. It **is** black.
7. My name **is** Bob.
8. They **are** nice girls.
9. The children **are** in the shop.
10. He **is** a teacher.
11. We **are** hungry.
12. Mrs Dixon **is** funny and nice.
13. I **am** twelve years old.
14. Jim and Cathy **are** at school.
15. The elephants **are** tired.
16. Mr Cooper **is** in the house.
17. The boys **are** in the park.
18. The mouse **is** in front of the hole.
19. Peter **is** a clever boy.
20. I **am** Sam.

FORMS OF "TO BE" 2

1. Mr Baker and I **are** friends.
2. It **is** time for dinner.
3. My name **is** Caroline.
4. My rabbit and my cat **are** friends.
5. They **are** very nice animals.
6. Dog food **is** also good for cats.
7. The children **are** in the garden.
8. Can I have an apple? Yes, here you **are**.
9. Mrs Dixon **is** funny and nice.
10. I **am** ten years old.
11. The weather **is** very nice today.
12. I **am** not tired.
13. This ball **is** very heavy.
14. The dogs **are** hungry. Let's feed them.
15. Look! Carol **is** at home.
16. This castle **is** very old.
17. My brother and I **are** good football players.
18. Ann **is** at the supermarket and her children **are** at school.
19. I **am** a student. My sister **is** a teacher.
20. How **are** you?

FORMS OF "TO BE" 3

1. Canada **isn't** a small country.
2. Ann **isn't** a nice girl.
3. My hands **aren't** cold.
4. They **aren't** tired.
5. He **isn't** a bad teacher.
6. I**'m not** at work.
7. She **isn't** at home in the morning.
8. We **aren't** in the park.
9. Jim **isn't** at school.
10. Our friends **aren't** on their summer holidays.
11. Uncle George **isn't** a good football player.
12. The dog **isn't** under the table.
13. He **isn't** very funny.
14. The shoes **aren't** white.
15. You **aren't** right.
16. Susan **isn't** good at tennis.
17. They **aren't** in the house.
18. His T-shirts **aren't** cool.
19. My sister **isn't** a good swimmer.
20. She **isn't** in Italy.

FORMS OF "TO BE" 4

1. **Are they** at school?
2. **Is she** lazy?
3. **Are the boys** good at school?
4. **Is Kevin** a good tennis player?
5. **Are the elephants** tired?
6. **Is Liam** good at sports?
7. **Is the book** on the desk?
8. **Are you** rich?
9. **Are his shoes** black?
10. **Are the cats** in the tree?
11. **Am I** late?
12. **Are they** busy?
13. **Is Pamela** pretty?
14. **Is the car** new?
15. **Is she** a nice girl?
16. **Are they** in the garden?
17. **Are my parents** at work?
18. **Is Tim** on holidays?
19. **Is it** a young cat?
20. **Are the books** in the schoolbag?

POSSESSIVE ADJECTIVES

Singular	Personal pronoun	Possessive adjective	Example
1st person	I	my	This is my phone.
2nd person	you	your	Is this your bike?
3rd person	he	his	This is his book.
	she	her	Her pullover is green.
	it	its	Here is its ball.

Plural			
1st person	we	our	We like our dog.
2nd person	you	your	Is this your car?
3rd person	they	their	This is their house.

POSSESSIVE ADJECTIVES 1

Fill in **my, your, his, her, its, our, their.**

1. Ann likes _____ teachers at school.

2. Is this Peter's book? No, _____ book is in the schoolbag.

3. Mary, is this _____ bike? No, _____ bike is behind the house.

4. The hamster is in _____ cage.

5. Henry helps _____ little brother.

6. Children, where are _____ exercise books?

7. The boys play with _____ football.

8. Tommy writes _____ homework.

9. Paul and Cathy eat _____ sandwiches.

10. My sister and I go to _____ grandmother.

11. The monkey eats _____ bananas.

12. The cats drink _____ milk.

13. Tom and I like spaghetti. It is _____ favourite food.

14. Carol and Bob don't like _____ classroom.

15. Can I play with _____ computer game, Tom?

16. Dad washes _____ car.

17. What's _____ telephone number, Susan?

18. Ann has two brothers. _____ names are Bill and George.

19. Lucy likes _____ new bike.

20. I can't find _____ new shirt.

POSSESSIVE ADJECTIVES 2

Fill in **my, your, his, her, its, our, their.**

1. I don't know the time because I can't find _____ watch.

2. What's the boy's name? _____ name is Ben Scott.

3. Debbie has got a cat. _____ cat is very lively.

4. The dog is very cute. _____ name is Ben.

5. We are at school. _____ school is very nice.

6. I have a new laptop. _____ laptop is white.

7. I'm from Seattle. Most of _____ friends are from Seattle, too.

8. The rabbit is white. _____ cage is in the garden.

9. Sandra and Jenny are friends. _____ school is in the city centre.

10. The Millers have a new car. _____ car is blue.

11. Emma Peel has got a brother. _____ name is Paul.

12. Nick Baker has a sister. _____ name is Debbie.

13. Yes, we have a dog. _____ dog is very old.

14. The boys have got a tortoise. _____ name is Trundle.

15. Suddenly the children see an old man. It's _____ grandfather.

16. Aunt Mary is sitting at the table. Peter fills _____ glass with juice.

17. We take the guitars and start to play. _____ music is great.

18. Mr Clark drives a yellow sports car. It's _____ car.

19. Tom and Robert like eating fish and chips. It's _____ favourite food.

20. We cannot come on Saturday. It's _____ father's birthday.

Complete English Grammar Rules

POSSESSIVE ADJECTIVES 3

Fill in **my, your, his, her, its, our, their.**

1. Can you spell _____ name?

2. Susan cannot find _____ pen.

3. Our uncle and aunt like _____ new house.

4. The cat is drinking _____ milk.

5. I must study for _____ test.

6. Peter is writing in _____ exercise book.

7. The children are writing _____ exams.

8. Carol likes _____ new skirt.

9. The dog is sleeping in _____ hut.

10. I often clean _____ bike.

11. The children sometimes clean _____ shoes.

12. The dogs eat _____ food.

13. We like _____ neighbours.

14. I cannot do _____ homework.

15. Sandra never always does _____ homework.

16. My brother always washes _____ new car on Sunday.

17. I need a pen. Can you lend me _____ pen?

18. Carol and Jane do not like _____ classroom because it's old.

19. Charles and Tom, when is _____ tennis match? I want to watch it.

20. We meet Drew and Mary in the circus. They are _____ friends.

POSSESSIVE ADJECTIVES 4

Fill in **my, your, his, her, its, our, their.**

1. Do you know where _____ keys are? I can't find _____.

2. I've lost _____ watch and I don't know where I've lost it.

3. Can you tell your sister that I've found _____ ring?

4. Kevin can't find _____ pencil case. Have you seen it?

5. I can't understand your argument, Caroline. Can you explain it?

6. Where have the boys been? We've been looking for _____ for hours.

7. This is _____ brother George. He's older than me.

8. We have two dogs. _____ names are Lupus and Sandy.

9. We have met before, but I can't remember _____ name.

10. We like Mrs Decker. _____ subjects are geography and English.

11. Larry and Ken, can I have _____ exercise books, please?

12. That's my friend Susan. _____ favourite sport is swimming.

13. We live in Arlington Road. _____ house is next to the school.

14. Look at my brother's hat. I think _____ colour is ugly.

15. He didn't like Patricia's essay about _____ holidays very much.

16. Peter, is this _____ dog which is always chasing _____ cat?

17. What a beautiful parrot! What's _____ name?

18. Mum usually helps my brothers with _____ homework.

19. _____ teacher is very nice. She often tells us funny stories.

20. I don't know Tom well, but I often talk to _____ sister.

Complete English Grammar Rules

POSSESSIVE ADJECTIVES 1

1. Ann likes **her** teachers at school.
2. Is this Peter's book? No, **his** book is in the schoolbag.
3. Mary, is this **your** bike? No, **my** bike is behind the house.
4. The hamster is in **its** cage.
5. Henry helps **his** little brother.
6. Children, where are **your** exercise books?
7. The boys play with **their** football.
8. Tommy writes **his** homework.
9. Paul and Cathy eat **their** sandwiches.
10. My sister and I go to **our** grandmother.
11. The monkey eats **its** bananas.
12. The cats drink **their** milk.
13. Tom and I like spaghetti. It is **our** favourite food.
14. Carol and Bob don't like **their** classroom.
15. Can I play with **your** computer game, Tom?
16. Dad washes **his** car.
17. What's **your** telephone number, Susan?
18. Ann has two brothers. **Their** names are Bill and George.
19. Lucy likes **her** new bike.
20. I can't find **my** new shirt.

POSSESSIVE ADJECTIVES 2

1. I don't know the time because I can't find **my** watch.
2. What's the boy's name? **His** name is Ben Scott.
3. Debbie has got a cat. **Her** cat is very lively.
4. The dog is very cute. **Its** name is Ben.
5. We are at school. **Our** school is very nice.
6. I have a new laptop. **My** laptop is white.
7. I'm from Seattle. Most of **my** friends are from Seattle, too.
8. The rabbit is white. **Its** cage is in the garden.
9. Sandra and Jenny are friends. **Their** school is in the city centre.
10. The Millers have a new car. **Their** car is blue.
11. Emma Peel has got a brother. **His** name is Paul.
12. Nick Baker has a sister. **Her** name is Debbie.
13. Yes, we have a dog. **Our** dog is very old.
14. The boys have got a tortoise. **Its** name is Trundle.
15. Suddenly the children see an old man. It's **their** grandfather.
16. Aunt Mary is sitting at the table. Peter fills **her** glass with juice.
17. We take the guitars and start to play. **Our** music is great.
18. Mr Clark drives a yellow sports car. It's **his** car.
19. Tom and Robert like eating fish and chips. It's **their** favourite food.
20. We cannot come on Saturday. It's **our** father's birthday.

POSSESSIVE ADJECTIVES 3

1. Can you spell **your** name?
2. Susan cannot find **her** pen.
3. Our uncle and aunt like **their** new house.
4. The cat is drinking **its** milk.
5. I must study for **my** test.
6. Peter is writing in **his** exercise book.
7. The children are writing **their** exams.
8. Carol likes **her** new skirt.
9. The dog is sleeping in **its** hut.
10. I often clean **my** bike.
11. The children sometimes clean **their** shoes.
12. The dogs eat **their** food.
13. We like **our** neighbours.
14. I cannot do **my** homework.
15. Sandra always does **her** homework.
16. My brother always washes **his** new car on Sunday.
17. I need a pen. Can you lend me **your** pen?
18. Carol and Jane do not like **their** classroom because it's old.
19. Charles and Tom, when is **your** tennis match? I want to watch it.
20. We meet Drew and Mary in the circus. They are **our** friends.

POSSESSIVE ADJECTIVES 4

1. Do you know where **my** keys are? I can't find **them**.
2. I've lost **my** watch and I don't know where I've lost it.
3. Can you tell your sister that I've found **her** ring?
4. Kevin can't find **his** pencil case. Have you seen it?
5. I can't understand **your** argument, Caroline. Can you explain it?
6. Where have the boys been? We've been looking for **them** for hours.
7. This is **my** brother George. He's older than me.
8. We have two dogs. **Their** names are Lupus and Sandy.
9. We have met before, but I can't remember **your** name.
10. We like Mrs Decker. **Her** subjects are geography and English.
11. Larry and Ken, can I have **your** exercise books, please?
12. That's **my** friend Susan. **Her** favourite sport is swimming.
13. We live in Arlington Road. **Our** house is next to the school.
14. Look at my brother's hat. I think **its** colour is ugly.
15. He didn't like Patricia's essay about **her** holidays very much.
16. Peter, is this **your** dog which is always chasing **my** cat?
17. What a beautiful parrot! What's **its** name?
18. Mum usually helps my brothers with **their** homework.
19. **Our** teacher is very nice. She often tells us funny stories.
20. I don't know Tom well, but I often talk to **his** sister.

A — AN

If you have to use a or an depends on the sound the word begins with.

If the first sound is a consonant, you have to use a.

	banana
a	sandwich
	girl

If the first sound is a vowel, you have to use an.

	apple
an	orange
	elephant

Note:
a uniform / a university - because the first letter starts with a "ju-sound".
an hour - because the first letter is silent, and the word starts with an "au-sound".

A — AN

Fill in **a** or **an**.

1. _____ apple

2. _____ ugly T - shirt

3. _____ hamster

4. _____ English book

5. _____ sweater

6. _____ iPad

7. _____ hamburger

8. _____ interview

9. _____ dog

10. _____ folder

11. _____ pen

12. _____ octopus

13. _____ uniform

14. _____ beautiful dress

15. _____ owl

16. _____ banana

17. _____ angry man

18. _____ box

19. _____ ice cream

20. _____ friend

21. _____ duck

22. _____ umbrella

23. _____ old house

24. _____ animal

25. _____ chair

26. _____ cheeseburger

27. _____ ox

28. _____ window

29. _____ table

30. _____ horse

31. _____ book

32. _____ elephant

33. _____ ant

34. _____ laptop

35. _____ internet server

36. _____ computer

37. _____ eraser

38. _____ pullover

39. _____ sofa

40. _____ exam

41. _____ schoolbag

42. _____ pot plant

43. _____ board

44. _____ eagle

45. _____ frog

46. _____ orange ball

47. _____ window

48. _____ woman

49. _____ ball

50. _____ door

A — AN

1.	**an** apple	26.	**a** cheeseburger
2.	**an** ugly T - shirt	27.	**an** ox
3.	**a** hamster	28.	**a** window
4.	**an** English book	29.	**a** table
5.	**a** sweater	30.	**a** horse
6.	**an** iPod	31.	**a** book
7.	**a** hamburger	32.	**an** elephant
8.	**an** interview	33.	**an** ant
9.	**a** dog	34.	**a** laptop
10.	**a** folder	35.	**an** internet server
11.	**a** pen	36.	**a** computer
12.	**an** octopus	37.	**an** eraser
13.	**a** uniform	38.	**a** pullover
14.	**a** beautiful dress	39.	**a** sofa
15.	**an** owl	40.	**an** exam
16.	**a** banana	41.	**a** schoolbag
17.	**an** angry man	42.	**a** pot plant
18.	**a** box	43.	**a** board
19.	**an** ice cream	44.	**an** eagle
20.	**a** friend	45.	**a** frog
21.	**a** duck	46.	**an** orange ball
22.	**an** umbrella	47.	**a** window
23.	**an** old house	48.	**a** woman
24.	**an** animal	49.	**a** ball
25.	**a** chair	50.	**a** door

A — AN — SOME

Singular: **a** or **an**

a banana   **a** cat   **a** monkey   **a** football

an egg   **an** orange   **an** umbrella   **an** eagle

Plural: **some**

some bananas   **some** cats   **some** monkeys   **some** footballs

some eggs   **some** oranges   **some** umbrellas   **some** eagles

Use **some** for things you **can't count**.

some milk   **some** tea   **some** water   **some** sugar

some coffee   **some** juice   **some** money   **some** butter

List of Common Uncountable Nouns

advice	gold	luck	silver
air	grass	luggage	snow
alcohol	ground	meat	space
art	happiness	milk	speed
beef	history	mist	steam
blood	homework	money	sugar
butter	honey	music	sunshine
cheese	hope	news	tea
chewing gum	ice	noise	tennis
chocolate	information	peanut butter	time
coffee	jam	pepper	toothpaste
confusion	juice	petrol	traffic
cotton	knowledge	plastic	trousers
education	lamb	pork	vinegar
electricity	lightning	power	washing up
entertainment	literature	pressure	washing up liquid
experience	love	rain	water
fiction	oil	rice	weather
flour	oxygen	sadness	wine
food	paper	salt	wood
forgiveness	patience	sand	wool
fresh air	pay	shopping	work
furniture	peace		

A — AN — SOME 1

Complete the sentences using either **a**, **an** or **some**.

1. There is _____ sand in my shoe.

2. There is _____ five-pound note in my wallet.

3. There is _____ wine in the cupboard.

4. There is _____ apple in the fridge.

5. There is _____ peanut butter on the worktop.

6. There is _____ radio in the kitchen.

7. There is _____ toothbrush in the bathroom.

8. There is _____ jam in the cupboard.

9. There is _____ magazine in the living room.

10. There is _____ queue at the post office.

11. There is _____ old bag in the car.

12. There is _____ suitcase in the bedroom.

13. There is _____ umbrella in the cupboard.

14. There is _____ sugar in your tea.

15. There is _____ bicycle outside.

16. There is _____ rice in the cupboard.

17. There is _____ dog in the garden.

18. There is _____ postman coming to the door.

19. There is _____ alcohol in the fridge.

20. There is _____ bathroom upstairs.

21. There is _____ computer in the office.

22. There is _____ oil on the floor.

23. There is _____ ice on the windscreen.

24. There is _____ shirt in the tumble dryer.

25. There is _____ homework to do later on.

26. There is _____ food on the table.

27. There is _____ egg in the fridge.

28. There is _____ light switch on the wall.

29. There is _____ vinegar on your chips.

30. There is _____ pen in my pocket.

A – AN – SOME 1

Complete the sentences using either **a**, **an** or **some**.

1. There is **some** sand in my shoe.

2. There is **a** five-pound note in my wallet.

3. There is **some** wine in the cupboard.

4. There is **an** apple in the fridge.

5. There is **some** peanut butter on the worktop.

6. There is **a** radio in the kitchen.

7. There is **a** toothbrush in the bathroom.

8. There is **some** jam in the cupboard.

9. There is **a** magazine in the living room.

10. There is **a** queue at the post office.

11. There is **an** old bag in the car.

12. There is **a** suitcase in the bedroom.

13. There is **an** umbrella in the cupboard.

14. There is **some** sugar in your tea.

15. There is **a** bicycle outside.

16. There is **some** rice in the cupboard.

17. There is **a** dog in the garden.

18. There is **a** postman coming to the door.

19. There is **some** alcohol in the fridge.

20. There is **a** bathroom upstairs.

21. There is **a** computer in the office.

22. There is **some** oil on the floor.

23. There is **some** ice on the windscreen.

24. There is **a** shirt in the tumble dryer.

25. There is **some** homework to do later on.

26. There is **some** food on the table.

27. There is **an** egg in the fridge.

28. There is **a** light switch on the wall.

29. There is **some** vinegar on your chips.

30. There is **a** pen in my pocket.

A – AN – SOME 2

Complete the sentences using either **a**, **an** or **some**.

1. Do you have _____ milk?

2. Would you like _____ cup of tea?

3. Do you want _____ orange?

4. Give him _____ present.

5. Father buys me _____ stickers.

6. Do you want _____ apple?

7. Have you got _____ stamps?

8. Would he like _____ orange juice?

9. Would you like _____ butter and jam?

10. Mum, please give me _____ melon.

11. The monkey eats _____ apple.

12. Tom reads _____ books every month.

13. This is _____ excellent test.

14. Please buy me _____ little hamster!

15. We need _____ eggs to bake _____ cake.

16. Would you like _____ coffee?

17. She invites _____ boys from her class once a month.

18. He always puts _____ sugar in his coffee.

19. Mum, I've got _____ letter for you.

20. I'd like _____ cornflakes, please.

A — AN — SOME 3

Complete the sentences using either a, an or some.

1. I have got _____ question.

2. We need _____ ice to cool the drinks.

3. There is _____ milk in the fridge.

4. Do you want _____ ice cream, Tom?

5. Please, buy _____ oranges. That's _____ good idea.

6. I want to buy _____ shirt and _____ pullover.

7. Jerry wants _____ toast for breakfast.

8. Bring _____ bottles of juice, please.

9. I'd like to have _____ roll and _____ tea for breakfast.

10. Buy _____ cheese for dinner, please.

11. He has _____ test every Friday.

12. Would you like _____ sweets?

13. He buys _____ orange.

14. Would you like _____ coffee?

15. She has got _____ stickers.

16. Do you have _____ raincoat?

17. We need _____ strawberries.

18. We go to _____ restaurant.

19. They have _____ exciting holiday.

20. She reads _____ book.

A — AN — SOME 4

Complete the sentences using either **a**, **an** or **some**.

1. Do you want _____ cup of coffee?

2. This is _____ American word.

3. This is _____ old book.

4. I'd like _____ cornflakes, please.

5. Please get _____ bread from the baker's.

6. There is _____ fly in the bottle.

7. Let's buy _____ new jeans.

8. Jerry gets _____ presents.

9. Can you give me _____ butter?

10. We need _____ more information from her.

11. That's _____ good idea to solve this problem.

12. She buys _____ skirt once a month.

13. She invites _____ boys and _____ girls to the party.

14. Does she have _____ paint box in her schoolbag?

15. He buys _____ oranges and _____ pineapple.

16. Let's go to the mall. I need _____ new coat.

17. I'll be back from shopping in _____ hour.

18. I need _____ new plants for my apartment.

19. Would you like _____ ice cream?

20. Her brother has _____ unusual pet.

A – AN – SOME 5

Complete the sentences using either **a**, **an** or **some**.

1. This is _____ important word.

2. Peter works in _____ office.

3. Give him _____ apples!

4. Would you like _____ toast?

5. He has _____ blue bike.

6. They have got _____ idea.

7. Can you lend me _____ money?

8. He is _____ policeman.

9. They have got _____ hamsters.

10. Can I have _____ apples, please?

11. Bill has got _____ orange snowboard.

12. This is _____ interesting story.

13. They like _____ hamburgers.

14. This is _____ expensive hotel.

15. Do you have _____ mobile phone?

16. She is _____ nice teacher.

17. We live in _____ old house.

18. He is _____ arrogant boy.

19. She is _____ beautiful girl.

20. We'll have _____ tests next week.

A — AN — SOME 6

Complete the sentences using either **a**, **an** or **some**.

1. Would you like to be _____ actress?

2. Sam always gives his wife _____ flowers on her birthday.

3. _____ birds, for example the penguin, cannot fly.

4. Those are _____ really nice trousers.

5. You need _____ visa to visit some foreign countries.

6. I'm going to the mall. I need _____ new clothes.

7. _____ shops are open on Sunday, but most are closed.

8. When I was _____ child, I didn't like rice.

9. I'm looking for _____ new job next month.

10. They bought _____ new laptops for the students.

11. They have _____ really nice flowerbeds in their garden.

12. My sister saw _____ accident when she went to school.

13. We live in _____ small flat in the centre of the city.

14. He usually reads _____ newspapers in the afternoon.

15. I found _____ $10 note on the pavement yesterday.

16. He sometimes writes _____ articles for a magazine.

17. She often wears black jeans and _____ orange T-shirt.

18. _____ children learn really very quickly.

19. Do you need _____ new notebook for school?

20. We go there once a year to spend _____ days on the beach.

A — AN — SOME 2

1. Do you have **some** milk?
2. Would you like **a** cup of tea?
3. Do you want **an** orange?
4. Give him **a** present.
5. Father buys me **some** stickers.
6. Do you want **an** apple?
7. Have you got **some** stamps?
8. Would he like **some** orange juice?
9. Would you like **some** butter and jam?
10. Mum, please give me **a** melon.
11. The monkey eats **an** apple.
12. Tom reads **some** books every month.
13. This is **an** excellent test.
14. Please buy me **a** little hamster!
15. We need **some** eggs to bake **a** cake.
16. Would you like **some** coffee?
17. She invites **some** boys from her class once a month.
18. He always puts **some** sugar in his coffee.
19. Mum, I've got **a** letter for you.
20. I'd like **some** cornflakes, please.

A — AN — SOME 3

1. I have got **a** question.
2. We need **some** ice to cool the drinks.
3. There is **some** milk in the fridge.
4. Do you want **an** ice cream, Tom?
5. Please, buy **some** oranges. That's **a** good idea.
6. I want to buy **a** shirt and **a** pullover.
7. Jerry wants **some** toast for breakfast.
8. Bring **some** bottles of juice, please.
9. I'd like to have **a** roll and **some** tea for breakfast.
10. Buy **some** cheese for dinner, please.
11. He has **a** test every Friday.
12. Would you like **some** sweets?
13. He buys **an** orange.
14. Would you like **some** coffee?
15. She has got **some** stickers.
16. Do you have **a** raincoat?
17. We need **some** strawberries.
18. We go to **a** restaurant.
19. They have **an** exciting holiday.
20. She reads **a** book.

A — AN — SOME 4

1. Do you want **a** cup of coffee?
2. This is **an** American word.
3. This is **an** old book.
4. I'd like **some** cornflakes, please.
5. Please get **some** bread at the baker's.
6. There is **a** fly in the bottle.
7. Let's buy **some** new jeans.
8. Jerry gets **some** presents.
9. Can you give me **some** butter?
10. We need **some** more information from her.
11. That's **a** good idea to solve this problem.
12. She buys **a** skirt once a month.
13. She invites **some** boys and **some** girls to the party.
14. Does she have **a** paintbox in her schoolbag?
15. He buys **some** oranges and **a** pineapple.
16. Let's go to the mall. I need **a** new coat.
17. I'll be back from shopping in **an** hour.
18. I need **some** new plants for my apartment.
19. Would you like **some** ice cream?
20. Her brother has **an** unusual pet.

A — AN — SOME 5

1. This is **an** important word.
2. Peter works in **an** office.
3. Give him **some** apples!
4. Would you like **some** toast?
5. He has **a** blue bike.
6. They have got **an** idea.
7. Can you lend me **some** money?
8. He is **a** policeman.
9. They have got **some** hamsters.
10. Can I have **an** apple, please?
11. Bill has got **an** orange snowboard.
12. This is **an** interesting story.
13. They like **some** hamburgers.
14. This is **an** expensive hotel.
15. Do you have **a** mobile phone?
16. She is **a** nice teacher.
17. We live in **an** old house.
18. He is **an** arrogant boy.
19. She is **a** beautiful girl.
20. We'll have **some** tests next week.

A — AN — SOME 6

1. Would you like to be **an** actress?
2. Sam always gives his wife **some** flowers on her birthday.
3. **Some** birds, for example the penguin, cannot fly.
4. Those are **some** really nice trousers.
5. You need **a** visa to visit some foreign countries.
6. I'm going to the mall. I need **some** new clothes.
7. **Some** shops are open on Sunday, but most are closed.
8. When I was **a** child, I didn't like rice.
9. I'm looking for **a** new job next month.
10. They bought **some** new laptops for the students.
11. They have **some** really nice flowerbeds in their garden.
12. My sister saw **an** accident when she went to school.
13. We live in **a** small flat in the centre of the city.
14. He usually reads **some** newspapers in the afternoon.
15. I found **a** $10 note on the pavement yesterday.
16. He sometimes writes **some** articles for a magazine.
17. She often wears black jeans and **an** orange T-shirt.
18. **Some** children learn really very quickly.
19. Do you need **a** new notebook for school?
20. We go there once a year to spend **some** days on the beach.

ADVERBS OF FREQUENCY

We use the adverbs of frequency to tell someone how often something happens:
Always= 100%, never = 0%

Frequency	Adverb
100%	always
90%	usually, regularly
80%	normally, generally
70%	often, frequently
50%	sometimes
30%	occasionally
10%	seldom
5%	rarely, hardly ever
0%	never

The position of the adverb of frequency in a sentence

The adverbs of frequency go **before a main verb**:

Subject + **adverb** + main verb or
Subject + auxiliary verb + **adverb** + main verb

We **never work** on Sundays.
They **usually play** volleyball on Thursdays.
I **always get up** at 7 during the week.
He can **usually visit** us on Sundays
We have **often got** some homework.

The adverbs of frequency go **after a form of to be** (am, is, are, etc.):

Subject + **to be** + adverb

They are **always** busy.
She was **often** late.

We can also use the following adverbs **at the beginning of a sentence**:
Usually, normally, often, frequently, sometimes, occasionally

Sometimes I go shopping on Saturdays.

ADVERBS OF FREQUENCY 1

Put the following sentences into correct order.

1. public / use / they / transport / usually

   _____

2. theatre / often / the / we / to / go

   _____

3. seldom / fish / dinner / has / he / for

   _____

4. read / frequently / my / the / papers / parents

   _____

5. sometimes / football / the / play / I / at / weekend / can

   _____

6. hands / always / meals / before / her / washes / she

   _____

7. for / late / work / is / Mary / never

   _____

8. the / watches / evenings / frequently / sister / my / in / TV

   _____

9. afternoon / shopping / Monday / hardly ever / on / go / a / they

   _____

10. I / up / rings / before / wake / sometimes / the / alarm

    _____

11. at / usually / time / workers / are / on / the / work

    _____

12. bed / before / brushes / her / she / going / teeth / to / always

    _____

13. a. / go / to / concert / seldom / out / see / we

    _____

14. restaurant / lunch / occasionally / have / in / a / they

    _____

15. up / dad / tea / has / cup / when / wakes / My / usually / first / he / of / a

ADVERBS OF FREQUENCY 1

Put the following sentences into correct order:

1. They usually use public transport.

2. We often go to the theatre.

3. He seldom has fish for dinner.

4. My parents frequently read the papers.

5. I sometimes play football at the weekend.

6. She always washes her hands before meals.

7. Mary is never late for work.

8. My sister frequently watches TV in the evenings.

9. They hardly ever go shopping on a Monday afternoon.

10. I sometimes wake up before the alarm rings.

11. The workers are usually at work on time.

12. She always brushes her teeth before going to bed.

13. We seldom go out to see a concert.

14. They occasionally have lunch in a restaurant.

15. My dad usually has a cup of tea when he first wakes up.

PRESENT TENSE SIMPLE

That's the way to express **habits, facts, thoughts and feelings**. It is used with **general statements** and actions that happen sometimes, always, usually or never.

Key words: all adverbs of frequency (often, always, never, usually, sometimes, generally, normally, rarely, seldom), every day, every month, whenever, on Mondays, on Tuesdays,...

past   present   future

How to form:

	Negation	Question
I, you, we, they	**don't** (do not) **+ verb**	**do + person + verb**
They go to school. I like oranges. We hate peppermint	They **don't go** to school. I **don't like** oranges. We **don't hate** peppermint.	Do they go to school? Do you like oranges? Do you hate peppermint?
he, she, it: verb + s	**doesn't** (does not) **+ verb**	**does + person + verb**
He wants a new car. She likes chips. It drinks milk.	He doesn't want a new car. She doesn't like chips. It doesn't drink milk.	Does he want a new car? Does she like chips? Does it drink milk?

NOTE:
-es after –s, -**ch**, -**sh**
pass – pass**es**, watch – watch**es**, finish – finish**es**

-**ies** if there is a consonant before the y
study – stud**ies**, carry – carr**ies**
but: play - play**s**

do – **does**, go – **goes**, have – **has**

NO verb + s with **can, may, might, must, should**

He should go home.   She can run fast.   It might be hungry.

PRESENT TENSE SIMPLE 1

Fill in the correct **present tense**.

1. Sarah and Pam _____ to the party. (go)

2. Jenny _____ Monica. (meet)

3. The children _____ in the garden. (play)

4. Sally _____ the board. (clean)

5. My sister _____ blue eyes. (have)

6. Bill _____ the window. (open)

7. Barbara _____ school uniforms look great. (think)

8. They all _____ dark blue pullovers. (wear)

9. My mum _____ shopping. (go)

10. I _____ hamburgers. (like)

11. He sometimes _____ a headache. (have)

12. They _____ a cold. (have)

13. She _____ at seven. (get up)

14. We _____ breakfast at eight. (have)

15. Peter _____ to school. (go)

16. Eric and Tom _____ home at two. (get)

17. He _____ an ice cream. (want)

18. I _____ peppermint. (hate)

19. My brother _____ TV. (watch)

20. She _____ her homework. (do)

PRESENT TENSE SIMPLE 2

Fill in the correct **present tense**.

1. Mary _____ stamps. (collect)

2. Tom and Sue _____ two comics. (buy)

3. Our friends often _____ football in the park. (play)

4. My mother _____ shopping every Friday. (go)

5. They always _____ in the first row. (sit)

6. She usually _____ Tom with the homework. (help)

7. My sister _____ in a big house. (live)

8. The children sometimes _____ hamburgers. (eat)

9. We often _____ about her. (talk)

10. Tom and Sue _____ cornflakes for breakfast. (like)

11. My parents often _____ westerns. (watch)

12. They _____ always hungry. (be)

13. Mum _____ all the dirty clothes on Saturday. (wash)

14. Dad _____ a new car every five years. (buy)

15. It _____ usually hot in summer. (be)

16. Mary always _____ her piano lesson on Fridays. (have)

17. He sometimes _____ in the library. (study)

18. She always _____ to work at seven o'clock. (go)

19. Bill and Tom sometimes _____ to London. (drive)

20. I _____ good at school. (be)

PRESENT TENSE SIMPLE 1

1. Sarah and Pam **go** to the party.
2. Jenny **meets** Monica.
3. The children **play** in the garden.
4. Sally **cleans** the board.
5. My sister **has** blue eyes.
6. Bill **opens** the window.
7. Barbara **thinks** school uniforms look great.
8. They all **wear** dark blue pullovers.
9. My mum **goes** shopping.
10. I **like** hamburgers.
11. He sometimes **has** a headache.
12. They **have** a cold.
13. She **gets up** at seven.
14. We **have** breakfast at eight.
15. Peter **goes** to school.
16. Eric and Tom **get** home at two.
17. He **wants** an ice cream.
18. I **hate** peppermint.
19. My brother **watches** TV.
20. She **does** her homework.

PRESENT TENSE SIMPLE 2

1. Mary **collects** stamps.
2. Tom and Sue **buy** two comics.
3. Our friends often **play** football in the park.
4. My mother **goes** shopping every Friday.
5. They always **sit** in the first row.
6. She usually **helps** Tom with the homework.
7. My sister **lives** in a big house.
8. The children sometimes **eat** hamburgers.
9. We often **talk** about her.
10. Tom and Sue **like** cornflakes for breakfast.
11. My parents often **watch** westerns.
12. They **are** always hungry.
13. Mum **washes** all the dirty clothes on Saturday.
14. Dad **buys** a new car every five years.
15. It **is** usually hot in summer.
16. Mary always **has** her piano lesson on Fridays.
17. He sometimes **studies** in the library.
18. She always **goes** to work at seven o'clock.
19. Bill and Tom sometimes **drive** to London.
20. I **am** good at school.

PRESENT SIMPLE NEGATION 1

Put the sentences into the negative form.

1. We have some milk. _____

2. Mother sews Jenny's jeans. _____

3. I hate maths lessons. _____

4. My brother likes eating oranges. _____

5. My parents often watch westerns. _____

6. Children like ice cream. Some _____

7. The monkey wants some bananas. _____

8. They are hungry. _____

9. We get up early on Sundays. _____

10. Peter is sometimes very tired. _____

11. I am a good pupil. _____

12. School always starts at seven o'clock. _____

13. Kate has her piano lesson on Mondays. _____

14. In summer it's sometimes very hot. _____

15. Mum washes all my dirty clothes. _____

16. Peter has got a brother. _____

17. The frog is under the caravan. _____

18. They are cool. _____

19. Dad buys a new car. _____

20. The boys play football. _____

PRESENT SIMPLE NEGATION 2

Put the sentences into the negative form.

1. I get up early. _____

2. Pamela watches TV. _____

3. Father has coffee. _____

4. I drink milk. _____

5. Robert has an idea. _____

6. We go to work. _____

7. He can come. _____

8. Mick opens the door. _____

9. Jim comes to the party. _____

10. The garden is full of flowers. _____

11. Peter helps in the kitchen. _____

12. Laura likes popcorn. _____

13. Phil's books are boring. _____

14. Mary plays with her friends. _____

15. They work in the garden. _____

16. She sings her favourite song. _____

17. Bill reads books. _____

18. The girls dance in her room. _____

19. He is in his office. _____

20. They do their homework. _____

PRESENT SIMPLE NEGATION 1

1. We **don't have** any milk.
2. Mother **doesn't sew** Jenny's jeans.
3. I **don't hate** maths lessons.
4. My brother **doesn't like** eating oranges.
5. My parents **don't** often **watch** westerns.
6. Some children **don't like** ice cream.
7. The monkey **doesn't want** some bananas.
8. They **aren't** hungry.
9. We **don't get** up early on Sundays.
10. Peter **isn't** sometimes very tired.
11. I **am not** a good pupil.
12. School **doesn't** always **start** at seven o'clock.
13. Kate **doesn't have** her piano lesson on Monday.
14. In summer it **isn't** sometimes very hot.
15. Mum **doesn't wash** all my dirty clothes.
16. Peter **hasn't got** a brother.
17. The frog **isn't** under the caravan.
18. They **aren't** cool.
19. Dad **doesn't buy** a new car.
20. The boys **don't play** football.

PRESENT SIMPLE NEGATION 2

1. I **don't get** up early.
2. Pamela **doesn't watch** TV.
3. Father **doesn't have** coffee.
4. I **don't drink** milk.
5. Robert **doesn't have** an idea.
6. We **don't go** to work.
7. He **cannot** (can't) come.
8. Mick **doesn't open** the door.
9. Jim **doesn't come** to the party.
10. The garden **isn't** full of flowers.
11. Peter **doesn't help** in the kitchen.
12. Laura **doesn't like** popcorn.
13. Phil's books **aren't** boring.
14. Mary **doesn't play** with her friends.
15. They **don't work** in the garden.
16. She **doesn't sing** her favourite song.
17. Bill **doesn't read** books.
18. The girls **don't dance** in her room.
19. He **isn't** in his office.
20. They **don't do** their homework.

PRESENT SIMPLE QUESTIONS 1

Form the questions of the following sentences.

Example: I am hungry. - Are you hungry?

1. Peter goes to the party.   _____

2. Mary can ski.   _____

3. I meet my friends.   _____

4. The teacher hands out the books.   _____

5. Pat is a clever boy.   _____

6. His schoolbag is brown.   _____

7. The monkey takes the banana.   _____

8. Tony is angry.   _____

9. Tim goes to school.   _____

10. They are at Sarah's party.   _____

11. He likes apples.   _____

12. Winter begins in December.   _____

13. They are at home.   _____

14. Tom can play football.   _____

15. His mother speaks Spanish.   _____

16. She wants an ice cream.   _____

17. Tamara likes sweets.   _____

18. Pam wants another T-shirt.   _____

19. I like black shoes.   _____

20. It is raining.   _____

PRESENT SIMPLE QUESTIONS 2

Form the questions of the following sentences.

Example: I am hungry. - Are you hungry?

1. They can dance. _____

2. I like reading books. _____

3. We live in a big city. _____

4. I can play the guitar. _____

5. They are cool. _____

6. We are friends. _____

7. The parrot eats apples. _____

8. They are Austrian. _____

9. We like our uncle. _____

10. Mary goes to the zoo. _____

11. Brad listens to the radio. _____

12. Elephants eat grass. _____

13. I am good at school. _____

14. They go to school by bus. _____

15. Henry does his homework. _____

16. Simon reads comics. _____

17. I like grey. _____

18. The window is open. _____

19. Mother likes butterflies. _____

20. Sam is happy. _____

PRESENT SIMPLE QUESTIONS 1

1. **Does Peter go** to the party?
2. **Can Mary ski**?
3. **Do you meet** your friends?
4. **Does the teacher hand out** the books?
5. **Is Pat** a clever boy?
6. **Is his schoolbag** brown?
7. **Does the monkey take** the banana?
8. **Is Tony** hungry?
9. **Does Tim go** to school?
10. **Are they** at Sarah's party?
11. **Does he like** apples?
12. **Does winter begin** in December?
13. **Are they** at home?
14. **Can Tom play** football?
15. **Does his mother speak** Spanish?
16. **Does she want** an ice cream?
17. **Does Tamara like** sweets?
18. **Does Pam want** another T-shirt?
19. **Do you like** black shoes?
20. **Is it** raining?

PRESENT SIMPLE QUESTIONS 2

1. **Can they** dance?
2. **Do you like** reading books?
3. **Do you live** in a big city?
4. **Can you play** the guitar?
5. **Are they** cool?
6. **Are you** friends?
7. **Does the parrot** eat apples?
8. **Are they** Austrian?
9. **Do you like** your uncle?
10. **Does Mary go** to the zoo?
11. **Does Brad listen** to the radio?
12. **Do elephants eat** grass?
13. **Are you good** at school?
14. **Do they go** to school by bus?
15. **Does Henry do** his homework?
16. **Does Simon read** comics?
17. **Do you like** grey?
18. **Is the window** open?
19. **Does mother like** butterflies?
20. **Is Sam** happy?

PRESENT SIMPLE QUESTIONS 3

(apple) Do you like apples?   😊   Yes, I do.

(apple) Do you like apples?   ☹   No, I don't.

(oranges) _____?   😊   _____

(tea) _____?   😊   _____

(ice cream) _____?   ☹   _____

(milk) _____?   😊   _____

(playing tennis) _____?   😊   _____

(weekends) _____?   😊   _____

(pink shoes) _____?   ☹   _____

(toffees) _____?   ☹   _____

(going to school) _____?   😊   _____

(chewing gums) _____?   😊   _____

(hamburgers) _____?   ☹   _____

(hot dogs) _____?   ☹   _____

(bananas) _____?   😊   _____

(fruit gums) _____?   ☹   _____

(cheeseburgers) _____?   😊   _____

(mascots) _____?   ☹   _____

(watching TV) _____?   😊   _____

(sandwiches) _____?   😊   _____

(reading) _____?   ☹   _____

(black T-shirts) _____?   ☹   _____

Complete English Grammar Rules

PRESENT SIMPLE 1

Write down the **negations** (N) and the **questions** (Q).

1. She likes ham and eggs.

   N: _____

   Q: _____

2. The weather is nice.

   N: _____

   Q: _____

3. My brother writes an email.

   N: _____

   Q: _____

4. They play the guitar.

   N: _____

   Q: _____

5. He runs fast.

   N: _____

   Q: _____

6. Pamela drives a new car.

   N: _____

   Q: _____

7. The boys are angry.

   N: _____

   Q: _____

8. This cat drinks milk.

   N: _____

   Q: _____

9. Peter is late.

   N: _____

   Q: _____

10. They sing beautifully.

    N: _____

    Q: _____

PRESENT SIMPLE 2

Write down the **negations** (N) and the **questions** (Q).

1. Samuel visits his uncle.   N: _____

                                   Q: _____

2. Pam leaves the house.   N: _____

                                   Q: _____

3. We hate spiders.   N: _____

                                   Q: _____

4. They are friendly.   N: _____

                                   Q: _____

5. Tina and Paul eat spaghetti.   N: _____

                                   Q: _____

6. He has a blue bike.   N: _____

                                   Q: _____

7. I understand.   N: _____

                                   Q: _____

8. His sister works hard.   N: _____

                                   Q: _____

9. They walk to school.   N: _____

                                   Q: _____

10. Gary and Peter go to the party. N: _____

                                   Q: _____

PRESENT SIMPLE 1

1. N: She **doesn't like** ham and eggs.
   Q: **Does she like** ham and eggs.
2. N: The weather **isn't** nice.
   Q: **Is the weather** nice?
3. N: My brother **doesn't write** an email.
   Q: **Does your brother write** an email?
4. N: They **don't play** the guitar.
   Q: **Do they play** the guitar?
5. N: He **doesn't run** fast.
   Q: **Does he run** fast?
6. N: Pamela **doesn't drive** a new car.
   Q: **Does Pamela drive** a new car?
7. N: The boys **aren't** angry.
   Q: **Are the boys** angry?
8. N: This cat **doesn't drink** milk.
   Q: **Does this cat drink** milk?
9. N: Peter **isn't** late.
   Q: **Is Peter** late?
10. N: They **don't sing** beautifully.
    Q: **Do they sing** beautifully.

PRESENT SIMPLE 2

1. N: Samuel **doesn't visit** his uncle.
   Q: **Does Samuel visit** his uncle?
2. N: Pam **doesn't leave** the house.
   Q: **Does Pam leave** the house?
3. N: We **don't hate** spiders.
   Q: **Do you hate** spiders?
4. N: They **aren't** friendly.
   Q: **Are they** friendly?
5. N: Tina and Paul **don't eat** spaghetti.
   Q: **Do Tina and Paul eat** spaghetti?
6. N: He **doesn't have** a blue bike.
   Q: **Does he have** a blue bike?
7. N: I **don't understand**.
   Q: **Do you understand**?
8. N: His sister **doesn't work** hard.
   Q: **Does his sister work** hard?
9. N: They **don't walk** to school.
   Q: **Do they walk** to school?
10. N: Gary and Peter **don't go** to the party.
    Q: **Do Gary and Peter go** to the party?

POSSESSIVE CASE

That's the way to express that someone owns something.

With **persons and animals**:

Singular: **'s**

This is Tom**'s** bike.

This is Kathy**'s** mother.

Plural: **s'**

These are the boy**s'** bikes.

This is the girl**s'** mum.

With **things**: **of**

The colour **of** the table is black.

The second chapter **of** this book.

If the noun **ends with an s**, add just the apostrophe to the end of the noun.

Where is Jes**s'** school bag?

If there are two nouns, change only the last one to the possessive.

Sam and Cathy**'s** new dog is really cute.

POSSESSIVE CASE 1

Use .... of ... / 's / s'

Examples: the door / the room   the door **of** the room
              the mother / Ann   Ann**'s** mother

1) the camera / Tom   _____

2) the eyes / the cat   _____

3) the top / the page   _____

4) the daughter / Charles   _____

5) the toys / the children   _____

6) the names / your friend   _____

7) the man / name   _____

8) the car / Mike   _____

9) the garden / our neighbours   _____

10) the birthday / my father   _____

11) the car / my parents   _____

12) the dog / the boys   _____

13) the dress / Susan   _____

14) the ball / the girls   _____

15) the price / the coat   _____

16) the ring / Chloe   _____

17) the rackets / the players   _____

18) the house / the Coopers   _____

19) the uncle / Bill   _____

20) the waiting room / the doctor   _____

POSSESSIVE CASE 1

1) Tom**'s** camera

2) the cat**'s** eyes

3) the top **of** the page

4) Charle**s'** daughter

5) the children**'s** toys

6) your friend**'s** names

7) the man**'s** name

8) Mike**'s** car

9) our neighbour**s'** garden

10) my father**'s** birthday

11) my parent**s'** car

12) the boy**s'** dog

13) Susan**'s** dress

14) the girl**s'** ball

15) the price **of** the coat

16) Chloe**'s** ring

17) the player**s'** rackets

18) the Cooper**s'** house

19) Bill**'s** uncle

20) the doctor**'s** waiting room

SHORT ANSWERS

FORMS OF TO BE – present tense

	Positive answers	Negative answers
Am I?	Yes, I am.	No, I'm not.
Are you?	Yes, you are.	No, you aren't.
Is he?	Yes, he is.	No, he isn't.
Is she?	Yes, she is.	No, she isn't.
Is it?	Yes, it is.	No, it isn't.
Are we?	Yes, we are.	No, we aren't
Are you?	Yes, you are.	No, you aren't.
Are they?	Yes, they are.	No, they aren't.

TO DO – present tense

	Positive answers	Negative answers
Do I?	Yes, I do.	No, I don't.
Do you?	Yes, you do.	No, you don't.
Does he?	Yes, he does.	No, he doesn't.
Does she?	Yes, she does.	No, she doesn't.
Does it?	Yes, it does.	No, it doesn't.
Do we?	Yes, we do.	No, we don't.
Do you?	Yes, you do.	No, you don't.
Do they?	Yes, they do.	No, they don't.

TO HAVE

	Positive answers	Negative answers
Have I got?	Yes, I have.	No, I haven't.
Have you got?	Yes, you have.	No, you haven't.
Has he got?	Yes, he has.	No, he hasn't.
Has she got?	Yes, she has.	No, she hasn't.
Has it got?	Yes, it has.	No, it hasn't.
Have we got?	Yes, we have.	No, we haven't.
Have you got?	Yes, you have.	No, you haven't.
Have they got?	Yes, they have.	No, they haven't.

CAN

	Positive answers	Negative answers
Can I?	Yes, I can.	No, I can't.
Can you?	Yes, you can.	No, you can't.
Can he?	Yes, he can.	No, he can't.
Can she?	Yes, she can.	No, she can't.
Can it?	Yes, it can.	No, it can't.
Can we?	Yes, we can.	No, we can't.
Can you?	Yes, you can.	No, you can't.
Can they?	Yes, they can.	No, they can't.

FORMS OF TO BE – past tense

	Positive answers	Negative answers
Was I?	Yes, I was.	No, I wasn't.
Were you?	Yes, you were.	No, you weren't.
Was he?	Yes, he was.	No, he wasn't.
Was she?	Yes, she was.	No, she wasn't.
Was it?	Yes, it was.	No, it wasn't.
Were we?	Yes, we were.	No, we weren't
Were you?	Yes, you were.	No, you weren't.
Were they?	Yes, they were.	No, they weren't.

TO DO – past tense

	Positive answers	Negative answers
Did I?	Yes, I did.	No, I didn't.
Did you?	Yes, you did.	No, you didn't.
Did he?	Yes, he did.	No, he didn't.
Did she?	Yes, she did.	No, she didn't.
Did it?	Yes, it did.	No, it didn't.
Did we?	Yes, we did.	No, we didn't.
Did you?	Yes, you did.	No, you didn't.
Did they?	Yes, they did.	No, they didn't.

SHORT ANSWERS 1

Write a positive (+) or negative (-) short answer next to the question.

1. Are you tired? (+) _____

2. Are the girls in the park? (-) _____

3. Is Carol your friend? (-) _____

4. Has Peter got a dog? (-) _____

5. Do you speak English? (+) _____

6. Are Jane and Nicky friends? (+) _____

7. Has Sam got a laptop? (-) _____

8. Can you walk to school? (+) _____

9. Does your mother make dinner? (+) _____

10. Do you read newspapers? (-) _____

11. Is this your pen? (-) _____

12. Can I help you? (+) _____

13. Do they like her? (-) _____

14. Are your parents at work? (+) _____

15. Can he play cricket? (-) _____

16. Does Scarlet like fish? (-) _____

17. Can he play chess? (+) _____

18. Is Mary from England? (+) _____

19. Are you from Germany? (-) _____

20. Have you got a car? (+) _____

SHORT ANSWERS 2

Write a positive (+) or negative (-) short answer next to the question.

1. Can you play the piano? (-) _____

2. Are the children in the garden? (-) _____

3. Does Steven come from Ireland? (+) _____

4. Is Mary tired? (-) _____

5. Has Peter got a pet? (-) _____

6. Are your students nice? (+) _____

7. Do you work hard? (+) _____

8. Can they visit me? (-) _____

9. Is it cold outside? (+) _____

10. Does it drink milk? (-) _____

11. Are the boys playing football? (+) _____

12. Do you like Sandra? (+) _____

13. Has she got a sister? (+) _____

14. Does he like lamb? (-) _____

15. Are you doing your homework? (+) _____

16. Is that your bike? (-) _____

17. Do you live in Dallas? (-) _____

18. Is he working in the garden? (-) _____

19. Are the children in the park? (+) _____

20. Can you take the dog for a walk? (+) _____

SHORT ANSWERS 3

Write a positive (+) or negative (-) short answer next to the question.

1. Are your friends good at sports?   (+)   _____

2. Did he phone you yesterday?   (-)   _____

3. Does she have a new laptop?   (-)   _____

4. Can she help you with the housework? (+)   _____

5. Was Angela ill last week?   (+)   _____

6. Do you have a webcam?   (-)   _____

7. Does he get any pocket money?   (+)   _____

8. Did he pass the exam?   (+)   _____

9. Can Sarah come to the party?   (-)   _____

10. Is your brother smart?   (+)   _____

11. Are they good at Maths?   (+)   _____

12. Did you watch the Super Bowl last weekend? (+)   _____

13. Were you in the shopping centre yesterday?   (-)   _____

14. Were they angry when you told them the truth? (-) _____

15. Are your parents at home at the moment?   (-)   _____

16. Did Ashley and Gabriel help you?   (-)   _____

17. Does your sister have a boyfriend?   (+)   _____

18. Did he come home late last night?   (-)   _____

19. Were they at the cinema yesterday?   (-)   _____

20. Have you ever been to South America?   (+)   _____

SHORT ANSWERS 4

Example: Is he married?   + Yes, he is.   — No, he isn't.

1. Did you watch the film last night?   + _____   — _____

2. Do whales have lungs?   + _____   — _____

3. Have they gone?   + _____   — _____

4. Can I have a lift into town?   + _____   — _____

5. Do you know my sister?   + _____   — _____

6. Does the bus leave in an hour?   + _____   — _____

7. Am I late?   + _____   — _____

8. Could they afford to move here?   + _____   — _____

9. Did Shakespeare live here?   + _____   — _____

10. Has Tommy told you his joke?   + _____   — _____

11. Will you wait for me?   + _____   — _____

12. Is it cold outside?   + _____   — _____

13. Would it be better to get a loan?   + _____   — _____

14. Are we going to the lake now?   + _____   — _____

15. Has she finished work yet?   + _____   — _____

16. Can I have a go on that game?   + _____   — _____

17. Is David's brother an accountant?   + _____   — _____

18. Will you get me a jar of coffee?   + _____   — _____

19. Are the team going to win?   + _____   — _____

20. Have you got a new jacket?   + _____   — _____

SHORT ANSWERS 1

1.	Are you tired?	**Yes, I am.**
2.	Are the girls in the park?	**No, they aren't.**
3.	Is Carol your friend?	**No, she isn't.**
4.	Has Peter got a dog?	**No, he hasn't.**
5.	Do you speak English?	**Yes, I do.**
6.	Are Jane and Nicky friends?	**Yes, they are.**
7.	Has Sam got a laptop?	**No, he hasn't.**
8.	Can you walk to school?	**Yes, I can.**
9.	Does your mother make dinner?	**Yes, she does.**
10.	Do you read newspapers?	**No, I don't.**
11.	Is this your pen?	**No, it isn't.**
12.	Can I help you?	**Yes, you can.**
13.	Do they like her?	**No, they don't.**
14.	Are your parents at work?	**Yes, they are.**
15.	Can he play cricket?	**No, he can't.**
16.	Does Scarlet like fish?	**No, she doesn't.**
17.	Can he play chess?	**Yes, he can.**
18.	Is Mary from England?	**Yes, she is.**
19.	Are you from Germany?	**No, I'm not.**
20.	Have you got a car?	**Yes, I have.**

SHORT ANSWERS 2

1.	Can you play the piano?	**No, I can't.**
2.	Are the children in the garden?	**No, they aren't.**
3.	Does Steven come from Ireland?	**Yes, he does.**
4.	Is Mary tired?	**No, she isn't.**
5.	Has Peter got a pet?	**No, he hasn't.**
6.	Are your students nice?	**Yes, they are.**
7.	Do you work hard?	**Yes, I do.**
8.	Can they visit me?	**No, they can't.**
9.	Is it cold outside?	**Yes, it is.**
10.	Does it drink milk?	**No, it doesn't.**
11.	Are the boys playing football?	**Yes, they are.**
12.	Do you like Sandra?	**Yes, I do.**
13.	Has she got a sister?	**Yes, she has.**
14.	Does he like lamb?	**No, he doesn't.**
15.	Are you doing your homework?	**Yes, I am.**
16.	Is that your bike?	**No, it isn't.**
17.	Do you live in Dallas?	**No, I don't.**
18.	Is he working in the garden?	**No, he isn't.**
19.	Are the children in the park?	**Yes, they are.**
20.	Can you take the dog for a walk?	**Yes, I can.**

SHORT ANSWERS 3

1.	Are your friends good at sports?	**Yes, they are.**
2.	Did he phone you yesterday?	**No, he didn't.**
3.	Does she have a new laptop?	**No, she doesn't.**
4.	Can she help you with the housework?	**Yes, she can.**
5.	Was Angela ill last week?	**Yes, she was.**
6.	Do you have a webcam?	**No, I haven't.**
7.	Does he get any pocket money?	**Yes, he does.**
8.	Did he pass the exam?	**Yes, he did.**
9.	Can Sarah come to the party?	**No, she can't.**
10.	Is your brother smart?	**Yes, he is.**
11.	Are they good at Maths?	**Yes, they are.**
12.	Did you watch the Super Bowl last weekend?	**Yes, I did.**
13.	Were you in the shopping centre yesterday?	**No, I wasn't.**
14.	Were they angry when you told them the truth?	**No, they weren't.**
15.	Are your parents at home at the moment?	**No, they aren't.**
16.	Did Ashley and Gabriel help you?	**No, they didn't.**
17.	Does your sister have a boyfriend?	**Yes, she does.**
18.	Did he come home late last night?	**No, he didn't.**
19.	Were they at the cinema yesterday?	**No, they weren't.**
20.	Have you ever been to South America?	**Yes, I have.**

SHORT ANSWERS 4

1.	Did you watch the film last night?	**+ Yes, I did.**	**— No, I didn't.**
2.	Do whales have lungs?	**+ Yes, they do.**	**— No, they don't.**
3.	Have they gone?	**+ Yes, they have.**	**— No, they haven't.**
4.	Can I have a lift into town?	**+ Yes, you can.**	**— No, you can't.**
5.	Do you know my sister?	**+ Yes, I do.**	**— No, I don't.**
6.	Does the bus leave in an hour?	**+ Yes, it does.**	**— No, it doesn't.**
7.	Am I late?	**+ Yes, you are.**	**— No, you aren't.**
8.	Could they afford to move here?	**+ Yes, they could.**	**— No, they couldn't.**
9.	Did Shakespeare live here?	**+ Yes, he did.**	**— No, he didn't.**
10.	Has Tommy told you his joke?	**+ Yes, he has.**	**— No, he hasn't.**
11.	Will you wait for me?	**+ Yes, I will.**	**— No, I won't.**
12.	Is it cold outside?	**+ Yes, it is.**	**— No, it isn't.**
13.	Would it be better to get a loan?	**+ Yes, it would.**	**— No, it wouldn't.**
14.	Are we going to the lake now?	**+ Yes, we are.**	**— No, we aren't.**
15.	Has she finished work yet?	**+ Yes, she has.**	**— No, she hasn't.**
16.	Can I have a go on that game?	**+ Yes, you can.**	**— No, you can't.**
17.	Is David's brother an accountant?	**+ Yes, he is.**	**— No, he isn't.**
18.	Will you get me a jar of coffee?	**+ Yes, I will.**	**— No, I won't.**
19.	Are the team going to win?	**+ Yes, they are.**	**— No, they aren't.**
20.	Have you got a new jacket?	**+ Yes, I have.**	**— No, I haven't.**

QUESTION TAGS

Question tags are used in spoken English, but not in written English. They are put at the end of the sentence.
To make a question tag, use the first auxiliary (forms of to be, have) or modal verb (must, can, will). If there isn't an auxiliary or modal verb, use do, does or did.

Positive or negative
If the sentence is positive, the question tag must be negative.

They **left** yesterday afternoon, **didn't** they?   He **is** good at dancing, **isn't** he?
She **was** surprised, **wasn't** she?

If the sentence is negative, the question tag must be positive.

They **didn't** leave yesterday, **did** they?   He **isn't** good at dancing, **is** he?
She **wasn't** surprised, **was** she?

Auxiliary verbs

They **haven't** met him before, **have** they?   He **is** in the park, **isn't** he?
They **are** studying at the moment, **aren't** they?   They **were** in Paris last week, **weren't** they?

Modal verbs

She **can** help him, **can't** she?   They **should** study for the test, **shouldn't** they?
He **will** tell me, **won't** he?   It **can't** be true, **can** it?

No auxiliary or modal verb

She **left** last Friday, **didn't** she?   He **works** in your company, **doesn't** he?
You **don't know** him, **do** you?

NOTE:
With I am you have to use "**aren't I**".
I am the best, **aren't I**?

She **has** a brother, **hasn't** she? (possession)   **BUT**   Peter has a terrible cold, **doesn't** he? (idiomatically)

There is a new restaurant next to your company, isn't **there**?
Let's go to the shopping mall, **shall** we?

Use the same auxiliary, modal verb or do, does or did to reply:

Your holidays **were** really relaxing, **weren't** they?   Yes, they **were**. We really enjoyed them.
She **visited** her aunt last week, **didn't** she?   Yes, she **did**. She went to her last Saturday.
You **couldn't** help him in the garden, **could** you?   No, I **couldn't**. I had to work in the office.

QUESTION TAGS 1

Write the correct question tag into the gaps.

1. You haven't got a car, _____?

2. Carol will be here soon, _____?

3. They weren't very relaxed, _____?

4. He doesn't like her, _____?

5. She is very attractive, _____?

6. You haven't seen my sister today, _____?

7. I'm late, _____?

8. Let's go for a walk, _____?

9. You aren't going to school today, _____?

10. They are on holidays, _____?

11. It's very expensive, _____?

12. You can play the drums, _____?

13. The movie was great, _____?

14. He couldn't remember, _____?

15. Tim, you don't know where Sandra is, _____?

16. It's raining, _____?

17. They are at home, _____?

18. It was a beautiful day, _____?

19. She works very hard, _____?

20. There is a station nearby, _____?

QUESTION TAGS 2

Write the correct question tag into the gaps.

1. You have enough money with you, _____?

2. She is looking after her younger brother, _____?

3. They stayed out late, _____?

4. You are talking about Pamela, _____?

5. He hasn't met her before, _____?

6. You won't tell my parents, _____?

7. She coloured her hair black, _____?

8. They weren't studying hard, _____?

9. He could give them a lift, _____?

10. She hasn't found the keys, _____?

11. The girls went shopping, _____?

12. It isn't a good restaurant, _____?

13. You don't want to walk home, _____?

14. They didn't like the movie, _____?

15. He bought a new laptop, _____?

16. You have two brothers and a sister, _____?

17. Let's go to the cinema, _____?

18. I'm too impolite, _____?

19. They are very smart, _____?

20. You tried on this jacket, _____?

QUESTION TAGS 3

Write the correct question tag into the gaps.

1. She hasn't got long, black hair, _____?

2. This blouse looks very nice, _____?

3. You should help her, _____?

4. They enjoyed their trip, _____?

5. It's going to rain, _____?

6. He lives in a small town, _____?

7. You had the flu last week, _____?

8. They moved to Berlin, _____?

9. Susan will help you, _____?

10. He has got a little dog, _____?

11. They came home late, _____?

12. You don't speak Spanish, _____?

13. She was there, _____?

14. He cooks well, _____?

15. They aren't at home, _____?

16. You like beef, _____?

17. I will see you again, _____?

18. They weren't angry, _____?

19. You didn't visit him, _____?

20. He wants to go on holidays, _____?

QUESTION TAGS 4

Write the correct question tag into the gaps.

1. Your parents will be here soon, _____?

2. That isn't your brother over there, _____?

3. You haven't got a laptop, _____?

4. He couldn't find a job, _____?

5. This is very pleasant, _____?

6. The hotel was excellent, _____?

7. They live in India, _____?

8. We should leave, _____?

9. There is a car park, _____?

10. They couldn't come to the meeting, _____?

11. She didn't buy a new car, _____?

12. You aren't a new student, _____?

13. Nice isn't in Italy, _____?

14. Carol wasn't at school last Monday, _____?

15. You can do it better, _____?

16. They are in Canada, _____?

17. She bought a new phone, _____?

18. The girls are in the garden, _____?

19. He isn't at home, _____?

20. Sandra is nice, _____?

QUESTION TAGS 5

Write the correct question tag into the gaps.

1. The others will be here in a minute, _____?

2. We mustn't forget to get some petrol, _____?

3. They can't stay for long, _____?

4. The course will be over in a week, _____?

5. We won't be back in the office until about one o'clock, _____?

6. She'll be late, _____?

7. We could go to the bank later, _____?

8. The program couldn't be installed on your PC, _____?

9. We couldn't book a room for two nights, _____?

10. I couldn't take you out for dinner tomorrow night, _____?

11. Lucy won't mind if I borrow her dress, _____?

12. The lasagne should be about ready by now, _____?

13. We should all meet up more often, _____?

14. Marco can drive us to the beach later, _____?

15. My phone can download any apps, _____?

16. We can't go swimming if the pool's shut, _____?

17. Gabriella won't let me use her hairdryer, _____?

18. Those girls can sing really well, _____?

19. Mandy shouldn't wear that much make-up, _____?

20. You couldn't give me a hand with the gardening, _____?

Complete English Grammar Rules

QUESTION TAGS 1

1. You haven't got a car, **have you**?
2. Carol will be here soon, **won't she**?
3. They weren't very relaxed, **were they**?
4. He doesn't like her, **does he**?
5. She is very attractive, **isn't she**?
6. You haven't seen my sister today, **have you**?
7. I'm late, **aren't I**?
8. Let's go for a walk, **shall we**?
9. You aren't going to school today, **are you**?
10. They are on holidays, **aren't they**?
11. It's very expensive, **isn't it**?
12. You can play the drums, **can't you**?
13. The movie was great, **wasn't it**?
14. He couldn't remember, **could he**?
15. Tim, you don't know where Sandra is, **do you**?
16. It's raining, **isn't it**?
17. They are at home, **aren't they**?
18. It was a beautiful day, **wasn't it**?
19. She works very hard, **doesn't she**?
20. There is a station nearby, **isn't there**?

QUESTION TAGS 2

1. You have enough money with you, **haven't you**?
2. She is looking after her younger brother, **isn't she**?
3. They stayed out late, **didn't they**?
4. You are talking about Pamela, **aren't you**?
5. He hasn't met her before, **has he**?
6. You won't tell my parents, **will you**?
7. She coloured her hair black, **didn't she**?
8. They weren't studying hard, **were they**?
9. He could give them a lift, **couldn't he**?
10. She hasn't found the keys, **has she**?
11. The girls went shopping, **didn't they**?
12. It isn't a good restaurant, **is it**?
13. You don't want to walk home, **do you**?
14. They didn't like the movie, **did they**?
15. He bought a new laptop, **didn't he**?
16. You have two brothers and a sister, **haven't you**?
17. Let's go to the cinema, **shall we**?
18. I'm too impolite, **aren't I**?
19. They are very smart, **aren't they**?
20. You tried on this jacket, **didn't you**?

QUESTION TAGS 3

1. She hasn't got long, black hair, **has she**?
2. This blouse looks very nice, **doesn't it**?
3. You should help her, **shouldn't you**?
4. They enjoyed their trip, **didn't they**?
5. It's going to rain, **isn't it**?
6. He lives in a small town, **doesn't he**?
7. You had the flu last week, **didn't you**?
8. They moved to Berlin, **didn't they**?
9. Susan will help you, **won't she**?
10. He has got a little dog, **hasn't he**?
11. They came home late, **didn't they**?
12. You don't speak Spanish, **do you**?
13. She was there, **wasn't she**?
14. He cooks well, **doesn't he**?
15. They aren't at home, **are they**?
16. You like beef, **don't you**?
17. I will see you again, **won't I**?
18. They weren't angry, **were they**?
19. You didn't visit him, **did you**?
20. He wants to go on holidays, **doesn't he**?

QUESTION TAGS 4

1. Your parents will be here soon, **won't they**?
2. That isn't your brother over there, **is it**?
3. You haven't got a laptop, **have you**?
4. He couldn't find a job, **could he**?
5. This is very pleasant, **isn't it**?
6. The hotel was excellent, **wasn't it**?
7. They live in India, **don't they**?
8. We should leave, **shouldn't we**?
9. There is a car park, **isn't there**?
10. They couldn't come to the meeting, **could they**?
11. She didn't buy a new car, **did she**?
12. You aren't a new student, **are you**?
13. Nice isn't in Italy, **is it**?
14. Carol wasn't at school last Monday, **was she**?
15. You can do it better, **can't you**?
16. They are in Canada, **aren't they**?
17. She bought a new phone, **didn't she**?
18. The girls are in the garden, **aren't they**?
19. He isn't at home, **is he**?
20. Sandra is nice, **isn't she**?

QUESTION TAGS 5

1. The others will be here in a minute, **won't they**?
2. We mustn't forget to get some petrol, **must we**?
3. They can't stay for long, **can they**?
4. The course will be over in a week, **won't it**?
5. We won't be back in the office until about one o'clock, **will we**?
6. She'll be late, **won't she?**
7. We could go to the bank later, **couldn't we?**
8. The program couldn't be installed on your PC, **could it**?
9. We couldn't book a room for two nights, **could we**?
10. I couldn't take you out for dinner tomorrow night, **could I**?
11. Lucy won't mind if I borrow her dress, **will she**?
12. The lasagne should be about ready by now, **shouldn't it**?
13. We should all meet up more often, **shouldn't we**?
14. Marco can drive us to the beach later, **can't he**?
15. My phone can download any apps, **can't it**?
16. We can't go swimming if the pool's shut, **can we**?
17. Gabriella won't let me use her hairdryer, **will she**?
18. Those girls can sing really well, **can't they**?
19. Mandy shouldn't wear that much make-up, **should she**?
20. You couldn't give me a hand with the gardening, **could you**?

QUESTION WORDS

WHAT	What is your name?
WHEN	When does he come?
WHERE	Where do you live?
WHY	Why are you late?
WHO	Who is that girl?
WHOSE	Whose pen is it?
WHICH	Which book do you like best?
HOW	How are you?
HOW MUCH	How much is the dress?
HOW MANY	How many computer games have you got?

Detailed information about the question words

Who - asking for a person and animal: subject: no do, does, did

Jane opened the door.	Who opened the door?
Tom helped in the garden.	Who helped in the garden?

Who - asking for a person and animal: object: do, does, did

They greet their teacher.	Who do they greet?
He asked Mary about the burglary.	Who did they ask about the burglary?

What - asking for a thing: subject: no do, does, did

His ankle hurt.	What hurts?
The flower pot fell on the floor.	What fell on the floor?

What - asking for a thing: object: do, does, did

She usually wears jeans.	What does she usually wear?
They built a castle in the sand.	What did they build in the sand?

Whose - asking for the 2nd case

This is Peter's pencil.	Whose pencil is this?
Carol's father was a drummer.	Whose father was a drummer?

When - asking for the time
I saw her <u>yesterday</u>.   When did you see her?
They came home <u>at midnight</u>.   When did they come home?

Where - asking for the place
He flew <u>to Manchester</u>.   Where did he fly?
He lives <u>in a big house</u>.   Where does he live?

Why - asking for a reason
He stayed at home <u>because he was ill</u>.   Why did he stay at home?
They like him <u>because he is always</u> friendly. Why do they like him?

How - asking for the manner (Art und Weise)
He drove <u>fast</u>.   How did he drive?
My holidays were <u>great</u>.   How were your holidays?

How long - asking for a period of time
They stayed there <u>for a week</u>.   How long did they stay there?
He lived in London <u>for a year</u>.   How long did he live in London?

How many - asking for an exact amount
In this factory work <u>500</u> people.   How many people work in this factory?
<u>50</u> kids were at his party.   How many kids were at his party?

How much - asking for not exact amount
He gets <u>10 pounds</u> pocket money a month.   How much pocket money does he get a month?
She bought <u>three bottles</u> of wine.   How much wine did she buy?

How often - asking for frequency
They play tennis <u>twice a week</u>.   How often do they play tennis?
She meets him <u>every Friday</u>.   How often does she meet him?

QUESTION WORDS 1

Complete the questions and find the answers – draw lines. Then write them down.

1. _____ book is it?   It's Kate.
2. _____ are my jeans?   It was fantastic.
3. _____ is Kate's birthday?   Peppermint.
4. _____ did you like the football match?   I think it's Mary's.
5. _____ is making the noise?   On Sunday.
6. _____ flavour is it?   They're in the cupboard.

_____

_____

_____

_____

_____

Complete the questions and find the answers – draw lines. Then write them down.

1. _____ is your favourite colour?   It's on Friday.
2. _____ is in the garden?   They're under the table.
3. _____ pencil is it?   The children.
4. _____ are you?   It's Peter's.
5. _____ are my shoes?   Orange.
6. _____ is your party?   I'm fine, thanks.

_____

_____

_____

_____

_____

Complete English Grammar Rules

QUESTIONS WORDS 2

Complete each sentence, using **what**, **where**, **when** or **how much**.

1. _____ colour is your new bike?   It's blue.

2. _____ were you born?   On May 21st.

3. _____ do you collect?   I collect stamps.

4. _____ are the boys?   In the park.

5. _____ does the film begin?   At 7.30.

6. _____ can we have a picnic?   I know a nice place near a pond.

7. _____ is the weather like in Chicago?   It's cold and windy.

8. _____ are the ski boots?   They are 380 pounds.

9. _____ do you usually have for breakfast?   I usually have toast and coffee.

10. _____ is your telephone number?   It's 4729147.

11. _____ do you have lunch?   At school.

12. _____ are your hobbies?   Skiing and tennis.

13. _____ colour is your car?   Red.

14. _____ is your mother?   She's in the garden.

15. _____ is your birthday?   In April.

16. _____ is an orange juice?   It's fifty pence.

17. _____ do you watch Tom and Jerry?   On Sunday at 9.

18. _____ are my shoes?   Under the bed.

19. _____ are the socks?   Three pounds 50.

20. _____ is your name?   Sarah.

QUESTIONS WORDS 3

Complete each sentence, using **what**, **where**, **when**, **who**, **how** or **how much**.

1. _____ sits next to Frank?   Clara.

2. _____ does the boy come from?   He's from Newcastle.

3. _____ is Peter's birthday?   In April, I think.

4. _____ is the shirt?   It's twenty pounds.

5. _____ is the best tennis player?   It's Bob.

6. _____ are you going?   I'm going to my friends.

7. _____ are you, Peter?   I'm fine, thanks.

8. _____ does the restaurant open?   It opens at six o' clock.

9. _____ can I get some ice cream?   You can get some at the snack bar.

10. _____ are you going to order?   Fish and chips.

11. _____ money have you left?   About 25 dollars.

12. _____ are you doing on Saturday? I don't know.

13. _____ has my pullover?   I have it.

14. _____ Is your name?   Carol.

15. _____ is Susan's party?   It's on Friday.

16. _____ are the potatoes?   They're one pound.

17. _____ old are you?   Twenty.

18. _____ do you live?   In Miami.

19. _____'s the time?   It's ten o'clock.

20. _____ is your mother?   She's doing some shopping.

Complete English Grammar Rules

QUESTIONS WORDS 4

Complete each sentence, using **what**, **where**, **when**, **who** or **why**.

1. _____'s the time please?   It's half past six.

2. _____ did he just say?   I'm sorry, I didn't listen.

3. _____ do you think you are?   Sorry for being impolite.

4. _____ is my coat?   On the clothes stand.

5. _____ do you want to leave?   This evening.

6. _____ didn't you go to college this morning? I was ill.

7. _____ was the Battle of Hastings?   In 1066.

8. _____ are you looking for?   I can't find my keys.

9. _____'s your name?   Brad.

10. _____ is the front door open?   I don't know.

11. _____ is the star of 'Spiderman'?   Sorry, but I didn't watch the movie.

12. _____ didn't you call me last night?   I left my phone in the office.

13. _____ do you live?   In Baltimore.

14. _____ did you go to last night?   At 9 o'clock.

15. _____ did you leave school?   In 1994.

16. _____ do you work?   In a bank.

17. _____ were you talking to yesterday?   To an old school friend.

18. _____'s going on?   That's really hard to explain.

19. _____ are you still in bed at four in the afternoon?   Because I've got a cold.

20. _____ is your birthday?   On April 14th.

QUESTIONS WORDS 5

Complete each sentence, using **what**, **where**, **when**, **who** or **whose**.

1. _____ can I get a newspaper?   You can get it round the corner.

2. _____ is your best friend?   It's Paul.

3. _____ does Nick live?   He lives in Boston.

4. _____ can speak French?   I think Stacy can.

5. _____ can I do for you?   I want two white T-shirts.

6. _____ book is this?   It's Nelly's.

7. _____ does Mr Olson live?   He lives in Market Street.

8. _____ can help me?   I can.

9. _____'s your favourite food?   I like roast beef best.

10. _____ does your mother get up?   At 7.

11. _____ pen is it?   It's Frank's.

12. _____ kind of films do you like best? Action films.

13. _____ is in the box?   Sweets, I guess.

14. _____ is that boy over there?   That's Simon Long.

15. _____ does the film start?   At 8.

16. _____ is his father's job?   He's a pilot.

17. _____ do you want to leave?   Early in the morning.

18. _____ has got a pencil for me?   Claudia has got one.

19. _____ are you doing tomorrow?   I've to work in the garden.

20. _____ car is that one over there?   It's my brother's.

QUESTIONS WORDS 6

Complete each sentence, using **what**, **where**, **when**, **who** or **why**.

1. _____ have I put my briefcase?   It's on the cupboard.

2. _____ were you talking to just now?   To my friend Caroline.

3. _____ is the baby crying?   It's hungry again.

4. _____ did you get home?   Late at night.

5. _____ are you so angry?   Because they have lost again.

6. _____ are we going to the park?   After lunch.

7. _____ time did they get home?   In the evening, at about 7.

8. _____ is the nearest post office?   Right behind the corner.

9. _____ do you come from?   I'm from Spain.

10. _____ shall I meet you after work?   At 6.

11. _____ did grandma say when you phoned her?   She enjoyed her trip to France.

12. _____ is your English teacher?   Mr Smith.

13. _____ have you painted your fence purple?   Because I like purple.

14. _____ shall I put this parcel?   Put it on the table.

15. _____ played football last night?   England vs. Germany.

16. _____ do you come home on Mondays?   Usually at 6.

17. _____ did you go to Munich?   Last year, in August.

18. _____ can't I find a good job?   I really don't know.

19. _____ is the best hockey player in your school?   It's Robert.

20. _____ are you late?   Because the bus was late.

QUESTIONS WORDS 7

Complete each sentence, using **what** or **which**.

1. _____ time do we have to be at school? At eight o'clock.

2. _____ languages does your father speak, French or Spanish?

3. _____ underground should we take? Line 3 or line 4?

4. _____ fruit do you like best? Bananas and mangoes.

5. _____ colour do you prefer, blue, orange or yellow?

6. _____ car do you like better, the VW or the Audi?

7. _____ is your favourite subject in school?

8. _____ hobbies does your sister have? She likes reading and sports.

9. _____ bus goes to the centre, number 30 or 31?

10. _____ arm did you break? I broke the left one.

11. _____ movie are you going to see? The new James Bond movie.

12. _____ can I do for you? I'd like to buy one of these shirts.

13. _____ of his children went to university? Frank studies economy.

14. _____ of his books won the Pulitzer Price? Her last one.

15. He said he left at nine _____ wasn't true.

16. _____ of your friends plays football best? Toni.

17. Can you tell me _____ the highest mountain is?

18. _____ do you feed your hamster? Corn and salad.

19. _____ of these statements is true? I think the second one.

20. _____ animal is the fastest? It's the cheetah.

Complete English Grammar Rules

QUESTIONS WORDS 1

Complete the questions and find the answers – draw lines. Then write them down.

1. **Whose** book is it?
2. **Where** are my jeans?
3. **When** is Kate's birthday?
4. **How** did you like the football match?
5. **Who** is making the noise?
6. **What** flavour is it?

I think it's Mary's.
They're in the cupboard.
On Sunday.
It was fantastic.
It's Kate.
Peppermint.

Complete the questions and find the answers – draw lines. Then write them down.

1. **What** is your favourite colour?
2. **Who** is in the garden?
3. **Whose** pencil is it?
4. **How** are you?
5. **Where** are my shoes?
6. **When** is your party?

Orange.
The children.
It's Peter's.
I'm fine, thanks.
They're under the table.
It's on Friday.

QUESTIONS WORDS 2

1. **What** colour is your new bike?
2. **When** were you born?
3. **What** do you collect?
4. **Where** are the boys?
5. **When** does the film begin?
6. **Where** can we have a picnic?
7. **What** is the weather like in Chicago?
8. **How much** are the ski boots?
9. **What** do you usually have for breakfast?
10. **What** is your telephone number?
11. **Where** do you have lunch?
12. **What** are your hobbies?
13. **What** colour is your car?
14. **Where** is your mother?
15. **When** is your birthday?
16. **How much** is an orange juice?
17. **When** do you watch Tom and Jerry?
18. **Where** are my shoes?
19. **How much** are the socks?
20. **What** is your name?

It's blue.
On May 21st.
I collect stamps.
In the park.
At 7.30.
I know a nice place near a pond.
It's cold and windy.
They are 380 pounds.
I usually have toast and coffee.
It's 4729147.
At school.
Skiing and tennis.
Red.
She's in the garden.
In April.
It's fifty pence.
On Sunday at 9.
Under the bed.
Three pounds 50.
Sarah.

QUESTIONS WORDS 3

1. **Who** sits next to Frank?   Clara.
2. **Where** does the boy come from?   He's from Newcastle.
3. **When** is Peter's birthday?   In April, I think.
4. **How much** is the shirt?   It's twenty pounds.
5. **Who** is the best tennis player?   It's Bob.
6. **Where** are you going?   I'm going to my friends.
7. **How** are you, Peter?   I'm fine, thanks.
8. **When** does the restaurant open?   It opens at six o' clock.
9. **Where** can I get some ice cream?   You can get some at the snack bar.
10. **What** are you going to order?   Fish and chips.
11. **How much** money have you left?   About 25 dollars.
12. **What** are you doing on Saturday?   I don't know.
13. **Who** has my pullover?   I have it.
14. **What** is your name?   Carol.
15. **When** is Susan's party?   It's on Friday.
16. **How much** are the potatoes?   They're one pound.
17. **How** old are you?   Twenty.
18. **Where** do you live?   In Miami.
19. **What**'s the time?   It's ten o'clock.
20. **Where** is your mother?   She's doing some shopping.

QUESTIONS WORDS 4

1. **What**'s the time please?   It's half past six.
2. **What** did he just say?   I'm sorry, I didn't listen.
3. **Who** do you think you are?   Sorry for being impolite.
4. **Where** is my coat?   On the clothes stand.
5. **When** do you want to leave?   This evening.
6. **Why** didn't you go to college this morning?   I was ill.
7. **When** was the Battle of Hastings?   In 1066.
8. **What** are you looking for?   I can't find my keys.
9. **What**'s your name?   Brad.
10. **Why** is the front door open?   I don't know.
11. **Who** is the star of 'Spiderman'?   Sorry, but I didn't watch the movie.
12. **Why** didn't you call me last night?   I left my phone in the office.
13. **Where** do you live?   In Baltimore.
14. **When** did you go to last night?   At 9 o'clock.
15. **When** did you leave school?   In 1994.
16. **Where** do you work?   In a bank.
17. **Who** were you talking to yesterday?   To an old school friend.
18. **What**'s going on?   That's really hard to explain.
19. **Why** are you still in bed at four in the afternoon?   Because I've got a cold.
20. **When** is your birthday?   On April 14th.

QUESTIONS WORDS 5

1.	**Where** can I get a newspaper?	You can get it round the corner.
2.	**Who** is your best friend?	It's Paul.
3.	**Where** does Nick live?	He lives in Boston.
4.	**Who** can speak French?	I think Stacy can.
5.	**What** can I do for you?	I want two white T-shirts.
6.	**Whose** book is this?	It's Nelly's.
7.	**Where** does Mr Olson live?	He lives in Market Street.
8.	**Who** can help me?	I can.
9.	**What**'s your favourite food?	I like roast beef best.
10.	**When** does your mother get up?	At 7.
11.	**Whose** pen is it?	It's Frank's.
12.	**What** kind of films do you like best?	Action films.
13.	**What** is in the box?	Sweets, I guess.
14.	**Who** is that boy over there?	That's Simon Long.
15.	**When** does the film start?	At 8.
16.	**What** is his father's job?	He's a pilot.
17.	**When** do you want to leave?	Early in the morning.
18.	**Who** has got a pencil for me?	Claudia has got one.
19.	**What** are you doing tomorrow?	I've to work in the garden.
20.	**Whose** car is that one over there?	It's my brother's.

QUESTIONS WORDS 6

1.	**Where** have I put my briefcase?	It's on the cupboard.
2.	**Who** were you talking to just now?	To my friend Caroline.
3.	**Why** is the baby crying?	It's hungry again.
4.	**When** did you get home?	Late at night.
5.	**Why** are you so angry?	Because they have lost again.
6.	**When** are we going to the park?	After lunch.
7.	**What** time did they get home?	In the evening, at about 7.
8.	**Where** is the nearest post office?	Right behind the corner.
9.	**Where** do you come from?	I'm from Spain.
10.	**When** shall I meet you after work?	At 6.
11.	**What** did grandma say when you phoned her?	She enjoyed her trip to France.
12.	**Who** is your English teacher?	Mr Smith.
13.	**Why** have you painted your fence purple?	Because I like purple.
14.	**Where** shall I put this parcel?	Put it on the table.
15.	**Who** played football last night?	England vs. Germany.
16.	**When** do you come home on Mondays?	Usually at 6.
17.	**When** did you go to Munich?	Last year, in August.
18.	**Why** can't I find a good job?	I really don't know.
19.	**Who** is the best hockey player in your school?	It's Robert.
20.	**Why** are you late?	Because the bus was late.

QUESTIONS WORDS 7

1. **What** time do we have to be at school? At eight o'clock.
2. **Which** languages does your father speak, French or Spanish?
3. **Which** underground should we take? Line 3 or line 4?
4. **What** fruit do you like best? Bananas and mangoes.
5. **Which** colour do you prefer, blue, orange or yellow?
6. **Which** car do you like better, the VW or the Audi?
7. **What** is your favourite subject in school?
8. **What** hobbies does your sister have? She likes reading and sports.
9. **Which** bus goes to the centre, number 30 or 31?
10. **Which** arm did you break? I broke the left one.
11. **What** movie are you going to see? The new James Bond movie.
12. **What** can I do for you? I'd like to buy one of these shirts.
13. **Which** of his children went to university? Frank studies economy.
14. **Which** of his books won the Pulitzer Price? Her last one.
15. He said he left at nine **which** wasn't true.
16. **Which** of your friends plays football best? Toni.
17. Can you tell me **what** the highest mountain is?
18. **What** do you feed your hamster? Corn and salad.
19. **Which** of these statements is true? I think the second one.
20. **What** animal is the fastest? It's the cheetah.

PERSONAL PRONOUNS

We use personal pronouns:

- ## to talk about ourselves

  I am happy that you can help **me**.
  We are very sad that you can't join **us**.

- ## to replace a noun we have used before

  Tom is my friend. **He** is very clever. I often play football with **him**.

- ## to address to other people (2nd person)

  Would **you** like some more coffee?
  I think Bob likes **you**.

- ## to introduce a remark (it)

  It was difficult to pass the test.
  It is hard to get up early in the morning.

- ## to talk about the weather, time, distance or temperature (it)

  It is raining.
  It is very cold today.
  It is 8 o'clock in the evening.

Singular	Subject	Object	Example
1st person	**I**	me	**I** need some help. Can you help me?
2nd person	**you**	you	Do **you** like milk? Carol likes you.
3rd person	**he**	him	**He** lives next to me. I often talk to him.
	she	her	**She** needs some help. Please help her.
	it	it	**It** was a difficult exam. Could you pass it?
Plural			
1st person	**we**	us	**We** are very glad that you can help us.
2nd person	**you**	you	Do **you** need a double room? Can I join you?
3rd person	**they**	them	**They** are thirsty. Give them some water, please.

PERSONAL PRONOUNS 1

Fill in the gaps using either **I** or **me.**

1. Give that book to _____.

2. _____ don't like working in shops.

3. Does your friend know _____?

4. Ted and _____ are going out for lunch.

5. _____ like strawberry milkshake best.

6. This is a picture of _____ and mum on holidays.

7. Did you know that _____ live in Manchester?

8. Jenny always tells _____ the truth.

9. Call _____ when you get there.

10. This is the house where _____ was born.

Fill in the gaps using either **we** or **us.**

1. _____ aren't interested.

2. They don't believe _____.

3. This is what _____ wanted.

4. They often see _____ walking down the road.

5. _____ agree with you.

6. Tell _____ what you mean.

7. Can _____ tell you tomorrow?

8. _____ don't want to go out.

9. This puts _____ in a difficult position.

10. That's impossible for _____.

PERSONAL PRONOUNS 2

Fill in the gaps using either **he** or **him**.

1. _____ always goes home early on Tuesdays.

2. Ask _____ for some help.

3. _____ is always a bit quiet.

4. That's easy for _____ to say.

5. Do you want to see _____ now?

6. _____ needs a new pair of shoes.

7. I think that _____ is really selfish.

8. Can you ask _____?

9. I love spending time with _____.

10. There's something strange about _____.

Fill in the gaps using either **she** or **her**.

1. _____ has got long hair.

2. I see _____ on the bus every day.

3. John usually calls _____ at half past nine.

4. Sally's sister often buys _____ a new jacket.

5. I know that _____ studies English.

6. _____'s quite serious, isn't she?

7. That guitar belongs to _____.

8. Is _____ going on holiday with you?

9. Ask my sister if _____ knows him.

10. _____ is not interested in geography.

PERSONAL PRONOUNS 3

Complete the sentences with **me, you, him, her, it, us, you** or **them**.

1. Who is that woman? Why are you looking at _____?

2. Do you know that man? Yes, I work with _____.

3. I am talking to you. Please listen to _____.

4. These photos are nice. Do you want to look at _____?

5. I like that camera. I am going to buy _____.

6. I don't know Peter's girlfriend. Do you know _____?

7. Where are the tickets? I can't find _____.

8. We are going to the disco. Can you come with _____?

9. I don't like dogs. I'm afraid of _____.

10. Where is she? I want to talk to _____.

11. Those apples are bad. Don't eat _____!

12. I don't know this girl. Do you know _____?

13. Alan never drinks milk. He doesn't like _____.

14. Where are the children? Have you seen _____?

15. I can't find my pencil. Can you give one to _____?

16. John can't do his homework. Can you help _____?

17. We don't know the way to the church. Can you help _____?

18. I can't find my books. Can you see _____?

19. John, can you come to _____?

20. This pen is for Mary. Give it to _____.

PERSONAL PRONOUNS 4

Complete the sentences with **me, you, him, her, it, us, you** or **them**.

1. We like to see the photos. Please show _____ to _____.

2. Mr Hoskins wants to read the newspaper. Please give _____ to _____.

3. Sam wants the eraser. Please give _____ to _____.

4. Your mother needs the camera. Please give _____ to _____.

5. My friends want to see your dogs. Please show _____ to _____.

6. I want to see your test. Please show _____ to _____.

7. We don't know your phone number. Please give _____ to _____.

8. I want those books. Please give _____ to _____.

9. He wants the key. Please give _____ to _____.

10. Carol wants the keys. Please give _____ to _____.

11. I want the laptop. Please give _____ to _____.

12. They want the money. Please give _____ to _____.

13. These flowers are a present for mother. Please, give _____ to _____.

14. This note is for father. Give _____ to _____.

15. This cake is for Carol and me. Please give _____ to _____.

16. The roses are for mother. Please give _____ to _____.

17. I need help. Please, help _____.

18. The boys are playing football. Give _____ the ball.

19. We are hungry. Bring _____ the sandwiches, please.

20. Father is in the living room. Bring _____ the book.

PERSONAL PRONOUNS 5

Complete the sentences with **me, you, him, her, it, us, you** or **them**.

1. My parents are very nice. They always help _____with my homework.

2. My friend Tom lives in London. This is a parcel from _____.

3. I'm sorry. I can't tell _____what happened.

4. The children are hungry. Give _____an apple.

5. We are thirsty. Can you give _____some juice?

6. Jack is in the garden. Bring _____his football.

7. Ann and Paul can't do their homework. Can you help _____?

8. I can't help _____tomorrow. I must visit my aunt.

9. These clothes are for poor children. Can you bring _____to the Red Cross?

10. Where is father? Can you tell _____where he is?

11. Where is the mouse? I can't see _____.

12. Where is the post office? Can you tell _____where it is?

13. What's your telephone number? I don't know _____.

14. Our brother is very nice. He always helps _____with the homework.

15. The children can see the cow. They can see _____.

16. Mike and I are in the garden. She can see _____.

17. I can't find my pen. Can you see _____?

18. I cannot help _____, Betty. I have other work to do.

19. My friend Susan lives in London. This is a postcard from _____.

20. The children are thirsty. Give _____a glass of water.

Complete English Grammar Rules

PERSONAL PRONOUNS 6

Complete the sentences with **me, you, him, her, it, us, you** or **them**.

1. Can you see Emma? No, I can't see _____.

2. Where are the pencils? I can't find _____.

3. John can't do his homework. Can you help _____?

4. We can't find the way to the church. Can you help _____?

5. I can't find my book. Can you see _____?

6. John, can you come to _____?

7. This book is for Jane. Please, give it to _____.

8. This cake is for Stephen and me. Please, give it to _____.

9. The roses are for father. Please, give them to _____.

10. I have got a problem with my maths homework. Can you help _____?

11. Here are the books. Read _____ in the holidays.

12. Would you like some more cake? No, I don't like the taste of _____.

13. Sam and Sally want to go home. Give _____ their coats.

14. Where is Mr Webster? I want to talk to _____.

15. I'm so thirsty. Please, give _____ a coke.

16. Where is Debbie? I can't find _____.

17. The football is not there. We have to look for _____.

18. We want to know where you were yesterday. Tell _____!

19. Are George and Linda here? I have a present for _____.

20. We are a big family. Mother always cooks for _____.

PERSONAL PRONOUNS 1

Fill in the gaps using either **I** or **me**.

1. Give that book to **me**.
2. **I** don't like working in shops.
3. Does your friend know **me**?
4. Ted and **I** are going out for lunch.
5. **I** like strawberry milkshake best.
6. This is a picture of **me** and mum on holidays.
7. Did you know that **I** live in Manchester?
8. Jenny always tells **me** the truth.
9. Call **me** when you get there.
10. This is the house where **I** was born.

Fill in the gaps using either **we** or **us**.

1. **We** aren't interested.
2. They don't believe **us**.
3. This is what **we** wanted.
4. They often see **us** walking down the road.
5. **We** agree with you.
6. Tell **us** what you mean.
7. Can **we** tell you tomorrow?
8. **We** don't want to go out.
9. This puts **us** in a difficult position.
10. That's impossible for **us**.

PERSONAL PRONOUNS 2

Fill in the gaps using either **he** or **him**.

1. **He** always goes home early on Tuesdays.
2. Ask **him** for some help.
3. **He** is always a bit quiet.
4. That's easy for **him** to say.
5. Do you want to see **him** now?
6. **He** needs a new pair of shoes.
7. I think that **he** is really selfish.
8. Can you ask **him**?
9. I love spending time with **him**.
10. There's something strange about **him**.

Fill in the gaps using either **she** or **her**.

1. **She** has got long hair.
2. I see **her** on the bus every day.
3. John usually calls **her** at half past nine.
4. Sally's sister often buys **her** a new jacket.
5. I know that **she** studies English.
6. **She**'s quite serious, isn't she?
7. That guitar belongs to **her**.
8. Is **she** going on holiday with you?
9. Ask my sister if **she** knows him.
10. **She** is not interested in geography.

PERSONAL PRONOUNS 3

1. Who is that woman? Why are you looking at **her**?
2. Do you know that man? Yes, I work with **him**.
3. I am talking to you. Please listen to **me**.
4. These photos are nice. Do you want to look at **them**?
5. I like that camera. I am going to buy **it**.
6. I don't know Peter's girlfriend. Do you know **her**?
7. Where are the tickets? I can't find **them**.
8. We are going to the disco. Can you come with **us**?
9. I don't like dogs. I'm afraid of **them**.
10. Where is she? I want to talk to **her**.
11. Those apples are bad. Don't eat **them**!
12. I don't know this girl. Do you know **her**?
13. Alan never drinks milk. He doesn't like **it**.
14. Where are the children? Have you seen **them**?
15. I can't find my pencil. Can you give one to **me**?
16. John can't do his homework. Can you help **him**?
17. We don't know the way to the church. Can you help **us**?
18. I can't find my books. Can you see **them**?
19. John, can you come to **me**?
20. This pen is for Mary. Give it to **her**.

PERSONAL PRONOUNS 4

1. We like to see the photos. Please show **them** to **us**.
2. Mr Hoskins wants to read the newspaper. Please give **it** to **him**.
3. Sam wants the eraser. Please give **it** to **him / her**.
4. Your mother needs the camera. Please give **it** to **her**.
5. My friends want to see your dogs. Please show **them** to **them**.
6. I want to see your test. Please show **it** to **me**.
7. We don't know your phone number. Please give **it** to **us**.
8. I want those books. Please give **them** to **me**.
9. He wants the key. Please give **it** to **him**.
10. Carol wants the keys. Please give **them** to **her**.
11. I want the laptop. Please give **it** to **me**.
12. They want the money. Please give **it** to **them**.
13. These flowers are a present for mother. Please, give **them** to **her**.
14. This note is for father. Give **it** to **him**.
15. This cake is for Carol and me. Please give **it** to **us**.
16. The roses are for mother. Please give **them** to **her**.
17. I need help. Please, help **me**.
18. The boys are playing football. Give **them** the ball.
19. We are hungry. Bring **us** the sandwiches, please.
20. Father is in the living room. Bring **him** the book.

PERSONAL PRONOUNS 5

1. My parents are very nice. They always help **me** with my homework.
2. My friend Tom lives in London. This is a parcel from **him**.
3. I'm sorry. I can't tell **you** what happened.
4. The children are hungry. Give **them** an apple.
5. We are thirsty. Can you give **us** some juice?
6. Jack is in the garden. Bring **him** his football.
7. Ann and Paul can't do their homework. Can you help **them**?
8. I can't help **you** tomorrow. I must visit my aunt.
9. These clothes are for poor children. Can you bring **them** to the Red Cross?
10. Where is father? Can you tell **me** where he is?
11. Where is the mouse? I can't see **it**.
12. Where is the post office? Can you tell **me** where it is?
13. What's your telephone number? I don't know **it**.
14. Our brother is very nice. He always helps **us** with the homework.
15. The children can see the cow. They can see **it**.
16. Mike and I are in the garden. She can see **us**.
17. I can't find my pen. Can you see **it**?
18. I cannot help **you**, Betty. I have other work to do.
19. My friend Susan lives in London. This is a postcard from **her**.
20. The children are thirsty. Give **them** a glass of water.

PERSONAL PRONOUNS 6

1. Can you see Emma? No, I can't see **her**.
2. Where are the pencils? I can't find **them**.
3. John can't do his homework. Can you help **him**?
4. We can't find the way to the church. Can you help **us**?
5. I can't find my book. Can you see **it**?
6. John, can you come to **me**?
7. This book is for Jane. Please, give it to **her**.
8. This cake is for Stephen and me. Please, give it to **us**.
9. The roses are for father. Please, give them to **him**.
10. I have got a problem with my maths homework. Can you help **me**?
11. Here are the books. Read **them** in the holidays.
12. Would you like some more cake? No, I don't like the taste of **it**.
13. Sam and Sally want to go home. Give **them** their coats.
14. Where is Mr Webster? I want to talk to **him**.
15. I'm so thirsty. Please, give **me** a coke.
16. Where is Debbie? I can't find **her**.
17. The football is not there. We have to look for **it**.
18. We want to know where you were yesterday. Tell **us**!
19. Are George and Linda here? I have a present for **them**.
20. We are a big family. Mother always cooks for **us**.

WHAT'S THE TIME?

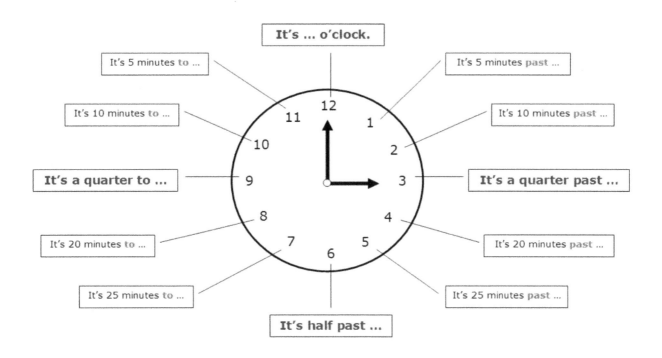

a.m. - p.m.

a.m. = ante meridiem = the time from midnight to noon = from 00:00 to 12:00
p.m. = post meridiem = the time from noon to midnight = from 12:00 to 24:00

The 24-hour clock is the most commonly used time notation in the world today.
But in English speaking countries the 12-hour clock is the dominant system of time written and spoken.
The 24-hour clock is only used by the military in the United States and Canada.

Examples:

24-hour	12-hour	
11:00	11 a.m.	It's eleven o'clock a.m.
23:00	11 p.m.	It's eleven o'clock p.m.
10:30	10.30 a.m.	It's half past ten a.m.
22:30	10:30 p.m.	It's half past ten p.m.
04:45	4:45 a.m.	It's a quarter to five a.m.
16:45	4:45 p.m.	It's a quarter to five p.m.
08:15	8:15 a.m.	It's a quarter past eight a.m.
20:15	8:15 p.m.	It's a quarter past eight p.m.
09:10	9:10 a.m.	It's ten (minutes) past nine a.m.
11:20	11:20 a.m.	It' twenty (minutes) past eleven a.m.
21:50	9:50 p.m.	It's ten (minutes) to ten p.m.
19:40	7:40 p.m.	It's twenty (minutes) to eight p.m.

WHAT'S THE TIME? 1

      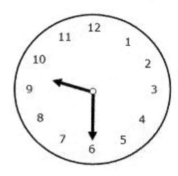

_____   _____   _____

_____   _____   _____

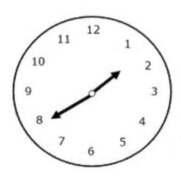      

_____   _____   _____

_____   _____   _____

      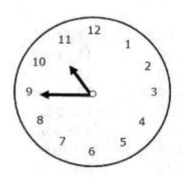

_____   _____   _____

_____   _____   _____

WHAT'S THE TIME? 2

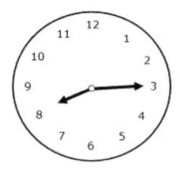

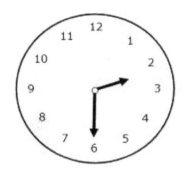

_____

_____

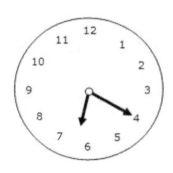

_____

_____

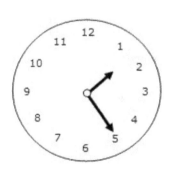

_____

_____

WHAT'S THE TIME? 3

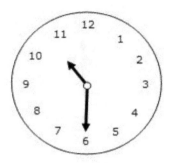

_____

_____

_____

_____

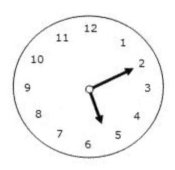

_____

_____

_____

_____

_____

_____

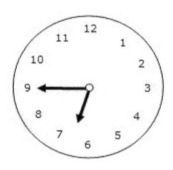

_____

_____

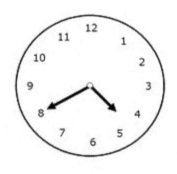

_____

_____

_____

_____

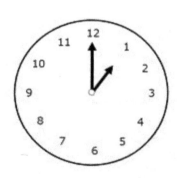

_____

_____

WHAT'S THE TIME? 4

Write down the times. Don't forget to write a.m. or p.m. Start the sentence with "It's".

1. 04:45 _____

2. 13:20 _____

3. 24:00 _____

4. 18:49 _____

5. 07:30 _____

6. 20:34 _____

7. 15:52 _____

8. 14:15 _____

9. 05:20 _____

10. 22:27 _____

11. 09:08 _____

12. 16:15 _____

13. 11:22 _____

14. 00:30 _____

15. 18:45 _____

16. 10:40 _____

17. 06:15 _____

18. 17:10 _____

19. 21:25 _____

20. 11:55 _____

WHAT'S THE TIME? 1

It's ten past three. It's a quarter past seven. It's half past nine.
It's twenty to two. It's five to five. It's twenty-five past one.
It's ten o'clock. It's five past six. It's a quarter to eleven.

WHAT'S THE TIME? 2

It's a quarter past eight. It's half past two. It's twelve o'clock. It's midnight. It's noon.
It's eight o'clock. It's ten to four. It's twenty past six.
It's a quarter to nine. It's a quarter past three. It's twenty-five past one.

WHAT'S THE TIME? 3

It's half past ten. It's five to twelve. It's ten past five.
It's twenty to eight. It's a quarter past two. It's a quarter to seven.
It's twenty to five. It's five past three. It's one o'clock.

WHAT'S THE TIME? 4

1. 04:45   It's a quarter to five a.m.
2. 13:20   It's twenty past one p.m.
3. 24:00   It's twelve o'clock p.m. It's midnight. It's twelve o'clock.
4. 18:49   It's eleven to seven p.m.
5. 07:30   It's half past seven a.m.
6. 20:34   It's twenty-six to nine p.m.
7. 15:52   It's eight to four p.m.
8. 14:15   It's a quarter past two p.m.
9. 05:20   It's twenty past five a.m.
10. 22:27   It's twenty-seven past ten p.m.
11. 09:08   It's eight past nine a.m.
12. 16:15   It's a quarter past four p.m.
13. 11:22   It's twenty-two past eleven a.m.
14. 00:30   It's half past twelve a.m. It's half past midnight.
15. 18:45   It's a quarter to seven p.m.
16. 10:40   It's twenty minutes to eleven a.m.
17. 06:15   It's a quarter past six a.m.
18. 17:10   It's ten past five p.m.
19. 21:25   It's twenty-five past nine p.m.
20. 11:55   It's five to twelve a.m. It's five to noon.

PRESENT PROGRESSIVE

The present progressive is also called **present continuous**.

How to form:	**Form of to be + verb + ing**		
	I	**am** + verb + ing	I **am playing**.
	he, she, it	**is** + verb + ing	The bird **is singing**.
	you, we, they	**are** + verb + ing	We **are dancing**.

The present progressive is used
- **to indicate actions happening at the time of speaking.**
- **for future actions that are planned.**

Key words: look, listen, now, at the moment, still, at present

Note:	take	taking	**no e**
	make	making	
	run	running	When a short vowel is spoken → **doubling of**
	sit	sitting	**the consonant**
	lie	lying	**ie → y**

Examples:	**Look**, Ann **is running** down the street.
	She **is sleeping now**.
	Listen, I'm **talking** to you!

For the **negation** use the negative form of the verb "to be".

Examples:	I'**m not watching** TV now.
	Look, she **isn't doing** her homework.
	They **aren't sleeping** at the moment.

Forming **questions: Form of to be – subject – main verb in the ing-form**

Examples:	**Are you cleaning** your room at the moment?
	What **is she doing** right now?
	Where **are they going**?

PRESENT PROGRESSIVE 1

Fill in the words from the box. Use the present progressive.

| play - work - sit - read - play - listen - clean - read |

Debbie and her friends _____ in Debbie's garden. They _____

football. Mrs Baker _____ a book. Mr _____ in the garden. Nick

_____ to his favourite CD. The cats _____ on Mrs Baker's chair.

Bill _____ his bike. Bill: "Debbie, help me, please." But Debbie is busy: "I

_____ a book for school. Ask your friend."

Fill in the words from the box. Use present progressive.

| play - listen - help - read - act - work – clean |

Sally and her friends _____ in the garden. They _____ for a

video. Her mother _____ a book. Her father _____ in the

garden. Dave _____ to a CD. Her brothers Ben and Frank _____

their bikes. Ben's friend _____ his mum in the garden.

PRESENT PROGRESSIVE 2

Write the present progressive into the gaps. Use the verb of the first sentence.

1. He sometimes goes to the park. Look, he _____ to the park.

2. She usually goes to school. Look, he _____ to school!

3. Liam often drinks a coffee. Right now, he _____ a coffee!

4. I swim every day. I _____ at the moment.

5. She washes her hair every day. She _____ her hair now.

6. The cat always drinks its milk. Look, it _____ its milk!

7. We never dance in the living room. We _____ in the living room now.

8. They never run to church. Look, they _____ to church!

9. You often write emails. Now, you _____ an email.

10. Mother cooks every day. Right now, mother _____ in the kitchen.

11. The monkey eats bananas. Look, the monkey _____ a banana!

12. In the afternoon we often watch TV. We _____ at the moment.

13. They usually have breakfast. Look, they _____ their breakfast!

14. Father usually drives a big car. At the moment father _____ a little red car.

15. The penguin swims very well. Look, the two little penguins _____!

16. The children often have their breakfast. The children _____ their breakfast now.

17. We often unload the dishwasher. Right now, we _____ the dishwasher.

18. I often play tennis with my friends. I _____ football at the moment.

19. He always sings in the shower. Listen, he _____ in the shower again.

20. We often have fish for lunch. Right now, we _____ beef.

PRESENT PROGRESSIVE 3

Write the present progressive into the gaps. Use the verbs in the brackets.

1. Andy _____ his uncle. (call)

2. Bill and Carol _____ a magazine. (read)

3. The boys _____ on the door. (knock)

4. Where is mum? She _____ the flowers in the garden. (water)

5. They _____ to their teacher. (not listen)

6. Why _____ you _____? (laugh)

7. _____ she _____ dinner? No, she is reading. (have - read)

8. We _____ now. (not play)

9. He _____ to his girlfriend at the moment. (talk)

10. Can we talk now? Yes, I _____ anything important. (not do)

11. Are you in the park? No, it _____. (rain)

12. What _____ the kids _____? They _____ their bikes. (do - ride)

13. Steven _____ a shower. (have)

14. Please be quieter. The babies _____. (sleep)

15. _____ you _____ the party? (enjoy)

16. I'm busy now because I _____ the house. (clean)

17. _____ they _____ lunch? (prepare)

18. The girls _____ an email to their friend. (write)

19. Her friends _____ in the park. (not play)

20. Do you have time to talk? Sorry, but I _____. (study)

Complete English Grammar Rules

PRESENT PROGRESSIVE 4

Write down the **negations** (N) and the **questions** (Q).

1. They are celebrating his birthday. N: _____

    Q: _____

2. Peter is phoning his friend.   N: _____

    Q: _____

3. He is wearing a green cap.   N: _____

    Q: _____

4. They are looking for the key.   N: _____

    Q: _____

5. The bus is coming.   N: _____

    Q: _____

6. He Is cleaning his teeth.   N: _____

    Q: _____

7. I am doing my homework.   N: _____

    Q: _____

8. I am talking to you.   N: _____

    Q: _____

9. They are dancing at the party.   N: _____

    Q: _____

10. She is opening her presents.   N: _____

    Q: _____

PRESENT PROGRESSIVE 1

Debbie and her friends **are playing** in Debbie's garden. They **are playing** football. Mrs Baker **is reading** a book. Mr Baker **is working** in the garden. Nick **is listening** to his favourite CD. The cats **are sitting** on Mrs Baker's chair. Bill **is cleaning** his bike. Bill: "Debbie, help me, please." But Debbie is busy: "I **am reading** a book for school. Ask your friend."

Sally and her friends **are playing** in the garden. They **are acting** for a video. Her mother **is reading** a book. Her father **is working** in the garden. Dave **is listening** to a CD. Her brothers Ben and Frank **are cleaning** their bikes. Ben's friend **is helping** his mum in the garden.

PRESENT PROGRESSIVE 2

1. He sometimes goes to the park. Look, he **is going** to the park.
2. She usually goes to school. Look, he **is going** to school!
3. Liam often drinks a coffee. Right now, he **is drinking** a coffee!
4. I swim every day. I **am swimming** at the moment.
5. She washes her hair every day. She **is washing** her hair now!
6. The cat always drinks its milk. Look, it **is drinking** its milk!
7. We never dance in the living room. We **are dancing** in the living room now.
8. They never run to church. Look, they **are running** to church!
9. You often write emails. Now, you **are writing** an email.
10. Mother cooks every day. Right now, mother **is cooking** in the kitchen.
11. The monkey eats bananas. Look, the monkey **is eating** a banana!
12. In the afternoon we often watch TV. We **are watching** at the moment.
13. They usually have breakfast. Look, they **are having** their breakfast!
14. Father usually drives a big car. At the moment father **is driving** a little red car.
15. The penguin swims very well. Look, the two little penguins **are swimming**!
16. The children often have their breakfast. The children **are having** their breakfast now.
17. We often unload the dishwasher. Right now, we **are unloading** the dishwasher.
18. I often play tennis with my friends. I **am playing** football at the moment.
19. He always sings in the shower. Listen, he **is singing** in the shower again.
20. We often have fish for lunch. Right now, we **are having** beef.

PRESENT PROGRESSIVE 3

1. Andy **is calling** his uncle.
2. Bill and Carol **are reading** a magazine.
3. The boys **are knocking** on the door.
4. Where is mum? She **is watering** the flowers in the garden.
5. They **aren't listening** to their teacher.
6. I **am doing** my homework now.
7. **Is** she **having** dinner? No, she **is reading**.
8. We **aren't playing** now.
9. He **is talking** to his girlfriend at the moment.
10. Can we talk now? Yes, I**'m not doing** anything important.
11. Are you in the park? No, it **is raining**.
12. What **are** the kids **doing**? They **are riding** their bikes.
13. Steven **is having** a shower.
14. Please be quieter. The babies **are sleeping**.
15. **Are** you **enjoying** the party?
16. I'm busy now because I **am cleaning** the house.
17. **Are** they **preparing** lunch?
18. The girls **are writing** an email to their friend.
19. Her friends **aren't playing** in the park.
20. Do you have time to talk? Sorry, but I **am studying**.

PRESENT PROGRESSIVE 4

1. N: They **aren't celebrating** his birthday.
   Q: **Are** they **celebrating** his birthday?
2. N: Peter **isn't phoning** his friend.
   Q: **Is** Peter **phoning** his friend?
3. N: He **isn't wearing** a green cap.
   Q: **Is** he **wearing** a green cap?
4. N: They **aren't looking** for the key.
   Q: **Are** they **looking** for the key?
5. N: The bus **isn't coming**.
   Q: **Is** the bus **coming**?
6. N: He **isn't cleaning** his teeth.
   Q: **Is** he **cleaning** his teeth?
7. N: I**'m not doing** my homework.
   Q: **Am** I **doing** my homework? **Are you doing** your homework?
8. N: I**'m not talking** to you.
   Q: **Am** I **talking** to you?
9. N: They **aren't dancing** at the party.
   Q: **Are** they **dancing** at the party?
10. N: She **isn't opening** her presents.
    Q: **Is** she **opening** her presents?

PRESENT PROGRESSIVE QUESTIONS 1

Complete the questions with the words in brackets. Use the present progressive.

Example: _____ the garden fence? (dad / paint) – Is dad painting the garden fence?

1. _____ the dishes? (mum / do)

2. _____ their favourite show? (the kids / watch)

3. _____ the lawn in his front yard? (Mr Jones / mow)

4. _____ us at the bus stop? (you / wait for)

5. _____ the new book? (Sandra / read)

6. _____ some milk? (the cats / drink)

7. _____? (your parents / still sleep)

8. _____ the beds right now? (Sam / make)

9. _____ breakfast? (the boys / have)

10. _____ football with his friends? (your brother / play)

11. _____ dinner at the moment? (dad / cook)

12. _____ for their exam? (the children / study)

13. _____ the garbage? (Carol / take out)

14. _____ shopping in the mall? (Susan and Anne / go)

15. _____ my brother again? (you / text)

16. _____ to music now? (Peter / listen)

17. _____ in the garden? (the men / barbecue)

18. _____ the neighbour's dog again? (our cat / chase)

19. _____ a cold? (your English teacher / have)

20. _____ in Chicago right now? (it / rain)

Complete English Grammar Rules

PRESENT PROGRESSIVE QUESTIONS 2

Change the following statements to questions. Pay attention to change pronouns and possessive adjectives like I, we, my, etc.

Example: I am doing my homework. Are you doing your homework?

1. Joan is having a shower. _____?

2. The girls are playing in the garden. _____?

3. We are studying for our French test. _____?

4. I am watching TV in the living room. _____?

5. My mother is cooking dinner. _____?

6. Our baby is sleeping right now. _____?

7. The boys are cleaning their bikes. _____?

8. The cat is eating its food. _____?

9. We are playing computer games now. _____?

10. Michael is meeting his friends. _____?

11. Amy is having her piano lesson. _____?

12. My sisters are baking cookies. _____?

13. Grandpa is going for a walk. _____?

14. Linda is singing in her room. _____?

15. I am doing my morning workout right now. _____?

16. The noise is coming from the garden shed. _____?

17. We are having lunch now. _____?

18. Dad is doing the shopping. _____?

19. My brothers are walking the dog. _____?

20. Nora is running to the bus station. _____?

PRESENT PROGRESSIVE QUESTIONS 1

1. **Is mum doing** the dishes?
2. **Are the kids watching** their favourite show?
3. **Is Mr Jones mowing** the lawn in his front yard?
4. **Are you waiting for** us at the bus stop?
5. **Is Sandra reading** the new book?
6. **Are the cats drinking** some milk?
7. **Are your parents still sleeping**?
8. **Is Sam making** the beds right now?
9. **Are the boys having** breakfast?
10. **Is your brother playing** football with his friends?
11. **Is dad cooking** dinner at the moment?
12. **Are the children studying** for their exam?
13. **Is Carol taking out** the garbage?
14. **Are Susan and Anne going** shopping in the mall?
15. **Are you texting** my brother again?
16. **Is Peter listening** to music now?
17. **Are the men barbecuing** in the garden?
18. **Is our cat chasing** the neighbour's dog again?
19. **Is your English teacher having** a cold?
20. **Is it raining** in Chicago right now?

PRESENT PROGRESSIVE QUESTIONS 2

1. Is Joan having a shower?
2. Are the girls playing in the garden?
3. Are you studying for your French test?
4. Are you watching TV in the living room?
5. Is your mother cooking dinner?
6. Is our baby sleeping right now?
7. Are the boys cleaning their bikes?
8. Is the cat eating its food?
9. Are you playing computer games now?
10. Is Michael meeting his friends?
11. Is Amy having her piano lesson?
12. Are your sisters baking cookies?
13. Is grandpa going for a walk?
14. Is Linda singing in her room?
15. Are you doing your morning workout right now?
16. Is the noise coming from the garden shed?
17. Are you having lunch now?
18. Is dad doing the shopping?
19. Are your brothers walking the dog?
20. Is Nora running to the bus station?

Present progressive negation 1

PRESENT PROGRESSIVE NEGATION

Make negative sentences in the present progressive tense. Use the verbs in brackets and the contracted forms ('m not, isn't, aren't).

1. Don't cheat, even if the teacher _____ at us. (look)

2. I want to lose weight. I_____ anything today. (eat)

3. The number of people without jobs _____ now. (rise)

4. Look out of the window. It _____ anymore. (snow)

5. They can help you because they _____ anymore. (work)

6. She _____ for her English test at the moment. (study)

7. Look, our dog _____ the cat today. (chase)

8. The twins _____ their breakfast. (have)

9. The children _____ TV right now. (watch)

10. I _____ my daily workout at the moment. (do)

11. The movie is funny, but Matt _____ it. (enjoy)

12. It's quiet. They _____ any noise. (make)

13. It's not cold today. That's why we _____ a jacket. (wear)

14. The population of our town _____ very fast. (rise)

15. Lucy still _____ better today. She must stay in bed. (feel)

16. His French wasn't very good, and it _____. (improve)

17. Tom and Jeff _____ tennis this season. (play)

18. Let's go out. It _____ anymore. (rain)

19. The kids are on the beach, but they _____ in the sea. (swim)

20. Well, I _____ now, but I'm very busy. (work)

PRESENT PROGRESSIVE NEGATION

Make negative sentences in the present progressive tense. Use the verbs in brackets and the contracted forms ('m not, isn't, aren't).

1. Don't cheat, even if the teacher **isn't looking** at us.
2. I want to lose weight. I**'m not eating** anything today.
3. The number of people without jobs **isn't rising** now.
4. Look out of the window. It **isn't snowing** anymore.
5. They can help you because they **aren't working** anymore.
6. She **isn't studying** for her English test at the moment.
7. Look, our dog **isn't chasing** the cat today.
8. The twins **aren't having** their breakfast.
9. The children **aren't watching** TV right now.
10. I**'m not doing** my daily workout at the moment.
11. The movie is funny, but Matt **isn't enjoying** it.
12. It's quiet. They **aren't making** any noise.
13. It's not cold today. That's why we **aren't wearing** a jacket.
14. The population of our town **isn't rising** very fast.
15. Lucy still **isn't feeling** better today. She must stay in bed.
16. His French wasn't very good, and it **isn't improving**.
17. Tom and Jeff **aren't playing** tennis this season.
18. Let's go out. It **isn't raining** anymore. (rain)
19. The kids are on the beach, but they **aren't swimming** in the sea. (swim)
20. Well, I**'m not working** now, but I'm very busy. (work)

PRESENT SIMPLE OR PROGRESSIVE

PRESENT SIMPLE

base form of the verb
(He, she, it: verb + 's')

I speak
you speak
he / she / it speaks
we speak
they speak

PRESENT PROGRESSIVE

Form of 'to be' + verb + ing

I am speaking
you are speaking
he / she / it is speaking
we are speaking
they are speaking

How to use

PRESENT SIMPLE

with habits, facts, thoughts, feelings and general statements

Colin plays football every Tuesday.

Sandra often watches TV.

PRESENT PROGRESSIVE

actions happening at the time of speaking

Look! Colin is playing football now.

They are watching TV at the moment.

Key words

All adverbs of frequency (often, always, never, usually, sometimes, generally, normally, rarely, seldom, ...)
every Sunday, every week, ...
whenever
on Mondays, on Tuesdays, ...

at the moment
at present
still
now
right now
Listen!
Look!

PRESENT SIMPLE OR PROGRESSIVE 1

Write the present simple or progressive into the gaps. Use the verbs in the brackets.

1. It's seven o'clock and they _____ to school now. (go)

2. Mrs Cooper _____ in the restaurant every Sunday. (eat)

3. Our cat never _____ on the kitchen table. (jump)

4. Look! The men _____ blue uniforms. (wear)

5. Curt always _____ his guitar in the afternoon. (play)

6. The taxi _____ for them at the moment. (wait)

7. He always _____ his grandmother in the coat. (help)

8. They never _____ very much. (eat)

9. Listen! Bill _____ his electric guitar. (play)

10. He _____ his car every Sunday. (wash)

11. The bell _____ at seven o'clock every morning. (ring)

12. They always _____ their aunt a tree for Christmas. (bring)

13. She _____ a red pullover and black jeans today. (wear)

14. The boys _____ snowballs at the girls now. (throw)

15. Mr Black _____ into the classroom at the moment. (walk)

16. Listen! The baby _____. (cry)

17. Sue sometimes _____ an egg for breakfast. (have)

18. We always _____ to school, but today we _____ the

    bus. (walk / take)

19. What are you doing? I _____ the dishes. (clean)

20. I never _____ beer. (drink)

PRESENT SIMPLE OR PROGRESSIVE 2

Write the present simple or progressive into the gaps. Use the verbs in the brackets.

1. Who _____ in the garden now? (play)

2. Look! I _____ a picture. (paint)

3. English children _____ French in their school. (learn)

4. Can you help me? No, sorry, I _____ for the test. (study)

5. Joe often _____ to school with me. (go)

6. It's nine o'clock and we _____ lunch now. (eat)

7. My sister never _____ table tennis. (play)

8. I always _____ breakfast at 7 o'clock. (eat)

9. Susan _____ TV now. (watch)

10. We _____ a book at this moment. (read)

11. Look! Pauline _____ the flowers. (water)

12. Listen! The girls _____ a song. (sing)

13. She usually _____ home by bus. (drive)

14. Jack _____ to his grandmother every day. (go)

15. Look! Sally and Joe _____ tennis. (play)

16. Nelly _____ a cup of tea every morning. (drink)

17. We can't play tennis. It _____ now. (rain)

18. Bill _____ his homework at the moment. (do)

19. Jane always _____ her homework in her room. (do)

20. The boys sometimes _____ in the park. (run)

PRESENT SIMPLE OR PROGRESSIVE 3

Write the present simple or progressive into the gaps. Use the verbs in the brackets.

1. My cat never _____ in my room. (sleep)

2. Listen! Phil _____ an English song. (sing)

3. No, I _____ to music, I _____ a bath. (not listen / have)

4. Michael can't play football. He _____ the guitar at the moment. (play)

5. We never _____ letters to our relatives in America. (write)

6. I never _____ of ghosts. (dream)

7. Tom _____ English in school. (learn)

8. Listen! Ann _____ the piano. (play)

9. What are you doing? I _____ a model plane. (make)

10. Can you help me? No, sorry, I _____ the baby. (look after)

11. Mum always _____ coffee in the afternoon. (drink)

12. Where is mum? She _____ dinner. (cook)

13. Who _____? This is Mr Blackwell. (speak)

14. We often _____ eggs for breakfast. (have)

15. What are you doing? I _____ for my English test. (study)

16. Tom _____ his bike at the moment. (clean)

17. He _____ his uncle every Wednesday. (visit)

18. What are you doing? I _____ TV. (watch)

19. Today it _____ (not rain), the sun _____. (shine)

20. They sometimes _____ to the cinema on Sundays. (go)

Complete English Grammar Rules

PRESENT SIMPLE OR PROGRESSIVE 4

Write the present simple or progressive into the gaps. Use the verbs in the brackets.

1. Would you like some beer? No, thank you I _____ alcohol. (not drink)

2. Why _____ Spanish? Because I want to go to Madrid next summer. (you study)

3. Where _____ from? (you come)

4. What _____ for a living? (your father do)

5. My sister _____ to be a nurse. (train)

6. That's an interesting article. It _____ you a lot about British teenagers. (tell)

7. What _____? A thriller. (you read)

8. Where _____ a ticket, please? (I get)

9. I don't like Mr Smith. He always _____ too much. (talk)

10. Susan, hurry up! What _____ in the bathroom all the time? (you do)

11. How _____ these days? (you get on)

12. What language _____ in Brazil? (they speak)

13. I think it _____ colder. We'd better take coats. (get)

14. Andy _____ like his brother, doesn't he? (look)

15. What's that noise? It _____ like a helicopter. (sound)

16. Most of the shops usually _____ at 9 o'clock. (open)

17. _____ the girls _____ TV at the moment? (watch)

18. He always _____ his breakfast at seven, and then he

_____ to work. (have / go)

19. Don't be so loud. Your little sister _____. (sleep)

20. She usually _____ computer games in the evening. (not play)

PRESENT SIMPLE OR PROGRESSIVE 1

1. It's seven o'clock and they **are going** to school now.
2. Mrs Cooper **eats** in the restaurant every Sunday.
3. Our cat never **jumps** on the kitchen table.
4. Look! The men **are wearing** blue uniforms.
5. Curt always **plays** his guitar in the afternoon.
6. The taxi **is waiting** for them at the moment.
7. He always **helps** his grandmother in the coat.
8. They never **eat** very much.
9. Listen! Bill **is playing** his electric guitar.
10. He **washes** his car every Sunday.
11. The bell **rings** at seven o'clock every morning.
12. They always **bring** their aunt a tree for Christmas.
13. She **is wearing** a red pullover and black jeans today.
14. The boys **are throwing** snowballs at the girls now.
15. Mr Black **is walking** into the classroom at the moment.
16. Listen! The baby **is crying**.
17. Sue sometimes **has** an egg for breakfast.
18. We always **walk** to school, but today we **are taking** the bus.
19. What are you doing? I **am cleaning** the dishes.
20. I never **drink** beer.

PRESENT SIMPLE OR PROGRESSIVE 2

1. Who **is playing** in the garden now?
2. Look! I **am painting** a picture.
3. English children **learn** French in their school.
4. Can you help me? No, sorry, I **am studying** for the test.
5. Joe often **goes** to school with me.
6. It's nine o'clock and we **are eating** lunch now.
7. My sister never **plays** table tennis.
8. I always **eat** breakfast at 7 o'clock.
9. Susan **is watching** TV now.
10. We **are reading** a book at this moment.
11. Look! Pauline **is watering** the flowers.
12. Listen! The girls **are singing** a song.
13. She usually **drives** home by bus.
14. Jack **goes** to his grandmother every day.
15. Look! Sally and Joe **are playing** tennis.
16. Nelly **drinks** a cup of tea every morning.
17. We can't play tennis. It **is raining** now.
18. Bill **is doing** his homework at the moment.
19. Jane always **does** her homework in her room.
20. The boys sometimes **run** in the park.

PRESENT SIMPLE OR PROGRESSIVE 3

1. My cat never **sleeps** in my room.
2. Listen! Phil **is singing** an English song.
3. No, I **am not listening** to music, I **am having** a bath.
4. Michael can't play football. He **is playing** the guitar at the moment.
5. We never **write** letters to our relatives in America.
6. I never **dream** of ghosts.
7. Tom **learns** English in school.
8. Listen! Ann **is playing** the piano.
9. What are you doing? I **am making** a model plane.
10. Can you help me? No, sorry, I **am looking after** the baby.
11. Mum always **drinks** coffee in the afternoon.
12. Where is mum? She **is cooking** dinner.
13. Who **is speaking**? This is Mr Blackwell.
14. We often **have** eggs for breakfast.
15. What are you doing? I **am studying** for my English test.
16. Tom **is cleaning** his bike at the moment.
17. He **visits** his uncle every Wednesday.
18. What are you doing? I **am watching** TV.
19. Today it **is not raining** (not rain), the sun **is shining**.
20. They sometimes **go** to the cinema on Sundays.

PRESENT SIMPLE OR PROGRESSIVE 4

1. Would you like some beer? No, thank you I **don't drink** alcohol.
2. Why **do you study** Spanish? Because I want to go to Madrid next summer.
3. Where **do you come** from?
4. What **does your father do** for a living?
5. My sister **is training** to be a nurse.
6. That's an interesting article. It **tells** you a lot about British teenagers.
7. What **are you reading**? A thriller.
8. Where **do I get** a ticket, please?
9. I don't like Mr Smith. He always **talks** too much.
10. Susan, hurry up! What **are you doing** in the bathroom all the time?
11. How **are you getting on** these days?
12. What language **do they speak** in Brazil?
13. I think it **is getting** colder. We'd better take coats.
14. Andy **looks** like his brother, doesn't he?
15. What's that noise? It **sounds** like a helicopter.
16. Most of the shops usually **open** at 9 o'clock.
17. **Are** the girls **watching** TV at the moment?
18. He always **has** his breakfast at seven, and then he **goes** to work.
19. Don't be so loud. Your little sister **is sleeping**.
20. She usually **doesn't play** computer games in the evening.